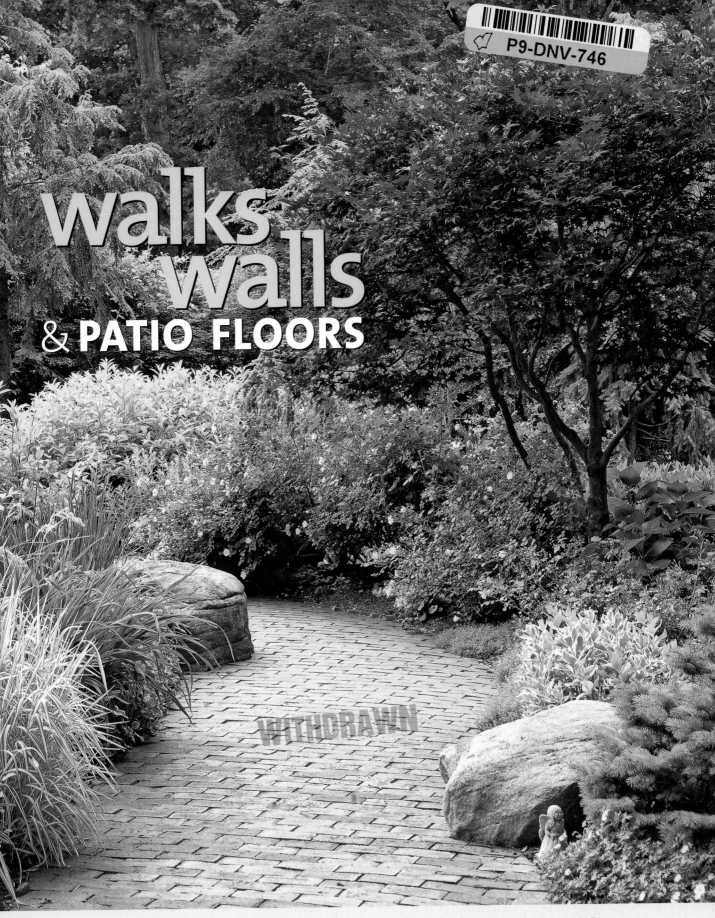

walks
walls
& PATIO FLOORS

by Jeanne Huber and the Editors of Sunset Books, Menlo Park, California

SUNSET BOOKS

VP, EDITORIAL DIRECTOR
Bob Doyle

DIRECTOR OF SALES
Brad Moses

DIRECTOR OF OPERATIONS
Rosann Sutherland

MARKETING MANAGER
Linda Barker

ART DIRECTOR
Vasken Guiragossian

STAFF FOR THIS BOOK

MANAGING EDITOR
Bridget Biscotti Bradley

COPY EDITOR
John Edmonds

PROOFREADER/INDEXER
Mary Pelletier-Hunyadi

PREPRESS COORDINATOR
Danielle Johnson

PRODUCTION SPECIALISTS
Linda M. Bouchard
Janie Farn

Cover: Photo by Roger Foley. Tom Mannion
Landscape Design.

For additional copies of *Walks, Walls & Patio Floors* or
any other Sunset book, visit us at www.sunsetbooks.com.

For more exciting home and garden ideas, visit
myhomeîdeas.com

contents

planning and materials

WALKS, WALLS, AND PATIO FLOORS PLAY A KEY ROLE IN HOME
LANDSCAPES. BESIDES SERVING AS DECORATIVE ELEMENTS, THEY
CREATE ORDER, MAKING GARDENS MORE USABLE. WALKS WELCOME
AND DIRECT PEOPLE, WALLS DELINEATE PUBLIC AND PRIVATE
AREAS, AND PATIOS CREATE OUTDOOR ROOMS FOR ENTERTAINING
AND LOUNGING. IN THIS CHAPTER, YOU'LL SEE INSPIRING
DESIGNS, LEARN ABOUT MATERIALS, AND GET DESIGN TIPS.

REWARDS OF GREAT DESIGN

WALKS, WALLS, AND PATIOS ARE CON-SIDERED HARDSCAPE, in contrast to the softscape of plants. While both are important, hardscape plays a bigger role in shaping how people use space. The projects featured in this book do this in many ways. They can break up an overly large yard and create intimate areas within it. They also work magic on yards that might seem too small to be useful. Add a wall for screening and put in a patio for a small table and chairs, and even a diminutive space suddenly becomes adequate for entertaining. Gardens equipped with walks, walls, and patios are also easier to care for than landscapes that consist of plants alone. These structural elements establish order, so a quick pass with a broom usually tidies up the space, whether or not the plants are perfectly groomed.

LEFT: Paved with gravel rather than covered with a standard lawn, a small yard functions as an easy-care outdoor living room. The bluestone trough serves as both a water feature and a hearth, thanks to gas and water pipes hidden within it.

LEFT: Color pulls together the different paving and wall materials used in this front-yard garden, which features slate paving and a natural stone wall, as well as concrete paving and block walls. The steps have an exposed aggregate finish, which means the surface is covered with pebbles that are embedded only partway into the concrete.

BELOW: To create a connection between indoors and out, the front patio on this house is paved with earth-toned concrete pavers that echo the interior floor.

FAR LEFT: The types of paving and wall material you select convey subtle messages about the role of different spaces. Flagstones surrounded by shredded bark have a more informal feel than the solid paving of the adjoining patio.

LEFT: Paving materials help define distinct areas of a landscape. In this yard, the brick walk widens next to the fountain. The paving then switches to bluestone and leads along a bed of hybrid tea roses to the sitting area beyond.

CHOOSING MATERIALS

ABOVE: **Bluestone pavers with mortar joints are supported underneath with a concrete pad. This kind of paving is the most expensive because you're paying for two layers, though you save a little on the top layer because the stone can be thinner than if it were set on sand or gravel. The concrete base keeps weeds from growing and makes cleanup a breeze. However, water can't seep through, so drainage becomes more critical. Also, from a DIY perspective, pouring concrete can be intimidating, at least the first time you do it.**

MASONRY MATERIALS USUALLY WORK BEST for paving garden surfaces and building garden walls. Although it's possible to build board-walk-style paths from wood, you'll find that ones of stone, brick, tile, and concrete usually last longer. They all look great in a garden too, because their solidity contrasts pleasantly with the soft texture of plants. There are pros and cons to every material.

For paths and patios, one of the main issues is whether to go with loose materials, individual pavers on sand or gravel, or a completely paved surface that includes a poured concrete slab. You can leave the concrete plain, decorate it, or use it as a base for mortared brick, stone, or tile. The cost escalates when you top concrete with another kind of paving, as you're paying for two layers. However, the cost of the concrete is partly offset by the savings in materials for the top layer, which can be thinner than it must be on a flexible base. On sand or gravel, pavers must be at least $1\frac{1}{2}$ inches thick. If they are as small as bricks, they should be even thicker, about $2\frac{1}{4}$ inches. But brick, tile, or stone installed in mortar over a concrete base can be as little as $\frac{1}{2}$ inch thick.

For walls, you'll also need to decide on a construction method before you buy materials. You have three options: build a dry-stacked wall, which consists of individual pieces; mortar the pieces together; or build a concrete-block wall and cover it with a veneer of thin stone, brick, or another material. If you want to build without mortar, select flat material, if possible, and try to get the largest pieces you can maneuver without hurting yourself, especially for the top row. Large pieces and hefty cap-stones result in stable walls. Mortared walls usually require more substantial foundations but allow you to build with smaller materials, such as bricks or even round river rock.

BELOW, LEFT: Mortar adds stability to this freestanding wall because it completely fills spaces between stones.

BELOW, RIGHT: For walls, block-shaped pieces are easiest to use, particularly if you are stacking them without mortar. To fill gaps, wedge in smaller stones, as was done with this low retaining wall, where creeping phlox *(Phlox subulata)* flows over the edge.

Paving with loose materials, such as gravel or bark, is easy and quick, and it costs the least. It's a good "green" option because water drains through, reducing storm-water runoff. But neighborhood cats may find it inviting, and there's a risk of tracking the material inside. One solution is to keep loose paving some distance from the house and switch to another material close to the door. In this garden, Indian basalt cobblestones were introduced little by little until they filled the entire path.

Natural Stone

For walks, walls, and patio floors, no material is more beautiful or durable than natural stone. Garden centers and home centers carry a limited array. You'll find a wider selection at stone yards and companies that specialize in masonry materials. Imported stone may catch your eye, but local stone probably costs less and may look more natural because it embodies a sense of place. It's also better environmentally, as less fuel is needed for transport.

Stone yards sell most material by the ton but price some pieces individually. Take dimensions of your project with you and ask the staff to help calculate how much you need. Buy at least 10 percent extra.

Flagstone is not a specific kind of stone but a general term referring to large, flat pieces $1/2$ to 4 inches thick. Most flagstone is sedimentary rock, which formed in layers and therefore naturally breaks into relatively flat pieces. Common types include sandstone, slate, quartzite, and limestone. Porous stone, including some sandstone, is likely to become covered with slippery moss if you use it in a shady spot in a damp climate. Flagstone is usually sold as paving and has a split surface that provides good traction. The relatively uniform thickness also makes it useful for walls, capstones, and veneer.

Stone tile is natural stone cut into squares or rectangles. Some types are cut as precisely as ceramic tiles, while others vary in thickness and width. Avoid polished stone tiles, which are too slippery for outdoor paving. Bluestone and slate with sawn or naturally split surfaces are among the most popular options. However, some slate isn't suitable for outdoor paving, especially in cold climates, so always ask the stone supplier. If you are choosing stone tile for a patio eating area, also ask whether you must seal the material to prevent food stains. Stone tile can also be used as capstones and veneer for walls.

Cobblestones, often made of granite, are roughly cut on the sides and have naturally rough tops. Some are cubes 4 or 5 inches on each side, while others are more like jumbo bricks up to 12 inches long. Cobblestones are thick and blocky, which helps them wedge together into stable paving or edging.

Rubble

Wall stone may be labeled with a bewildering array of names. Fieldstone, rubble, boulders, and river rock are all terms for pieces with random shapes. Fieldstone, which literally means stone found in a field, may have bits of lichen or moss, which adds instant patina to walls. Rubble has an irregular shape, so it takes skill to use it for walls. Semi-dresssed stone, which is roughly flat on two sides, is easier to use. Fully trimmed stone, often called ashlar, is more block-shaped. In a coursed ashlar design (pictured here), each row has stones the same height. Random and combination ashlar walls combine stones of various heights.

Semi-dressed stone

Ashlar stone

Veneer stone is made for layering over walls built of concrete block, poured concrete, or even wood (provided you add a moisture barrier and metal mesh first). Standard stone veneer, which may be several inches thick, needs to be supported by a foundation or a metal angle iron bolted to the wall. Thin veneer, which may be just $1/2$ or $3/4$ inch thick, is light enough that it needs no foundation. You just mortar pieces to the wall, much as you might install tile. Some stone companies sell corner pieces that hide the thin edges of the veneer (pictured at left). The pieces come with long and short ends so you can alternate the orientation as you add courses.

You may also find artificial stone veneer, made with portland cement and pumice. It doesn't need a foundation either, and it's even easier to install. But a trained eye can tell it's not as bright or textured as the real thing. Artificial stone may cost more than real stone veneer, though the total installed cost might be lower because of the labor savings.

DESIGN TIP

Bricks may be shades of red, yellow, or gray. Wall bricks often have additional color on the sides and ends, the only surfaces that show in a wall.

Brick

Brick has a timeless beauty, with baked-in color that will never fade. Many patterns are possible, and building with brick takes little strength, as each piece fits comfortably in one hand.

Bricks are made of clay or shale. Although some are still pressed into molds, most bricks today are extruded from machines that resemble Play-Doh Fun Factory toys. The bricks are then heated in a kiln. The higher the temperature, the less porous the bricks become. This increases their frost resistance, since bricks crumble when water in them freezes and expands. You can use bricks rated SX or SW (for severe weathering) anywhere. Use MX or MW (moderate weathering) bricks only in warm climates or possibly for walls in areas where temperatures dip below freezing only occasionally. NW (negligible weathering) bricks are for interior use only. There is no downside to using SW bricks for all applications, so many manufacturers simplify by selling only these. Do check, though. Your local building inspector can tell you what's required in your area.

Paving bricks are always solid. They come in two basic categories. Standard bricks are sold by their actual dimensions, usually 4 by 8 by 2¼ inches. Use them for paving where pieces have only about ⅛ inch of sand between joints. They're also good edging pieces for paths or patios. If you intend to use mortar between joints, buy modular-size bricks, which are typically 3⅝ by 7⅝ inches on the top and bottom so you can have ⅜-inch-wide mortar joints and still get patterns to line up correctly. These bricks feature slightly rounded, or chamfered, edges, which add slip resistance and allow water to drain better.

Standard brick   Modular-size brick

The one pictured has a white surface coating. Most traditional patterns are based on the assumption that a brick's width, or effective width including mortar, is half its length.

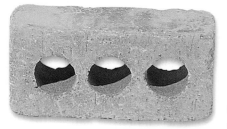

Wall bricks, also known as facing bricks, may be solid or cored, with several holes in the center. The holes cut down on weight and raw materials, but their main purpose is to ensure stronger walls. The mortar between layers oozes up and down into the holes, helping to lock pieces together.

In walls, use solid bricks only for the top course, or for low garden walls or planters that don't need much strength. Wall bricks are sold only in modular dimensions, as walls always need mortar.

Brick veneer is a type of thin brick designed to be added to walls built of concrete block, poured concrete, or even wood. Unlike the thin bricks made for paving, veneer pieces are cut to expose the side dimension so the finished wall looks as it would if it were built of solid brick. Some manufacturers make special corner pieces that hide the thin edge of the veneer (shown at right). These cost more than standard bricks because there are more manufacturing steps.

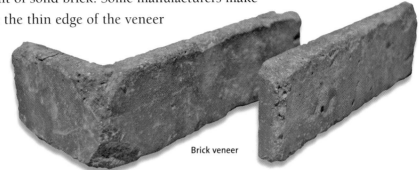

Brick veneer

Concrete bricks

Concrete bricks are tinted and molded to look like clay bricks. They cost less and can be used in the same ways as clay-based bricks. However, clay bricks retain their color, while concrete bricks may lighten in time. Also, sand in the concrete mix may become exposed, changing the look.

Used Bricks

Used bricks, which often have bits of mortar stuck to the surface, add a pleasantly rustic look to garden projects. But be careful about what you use. Some used bricks weren't made to be out in the weather, particularly as paving. Mortar bits on all faces are clues that bricks were inside a wall; they're probably not weatherproof. But if the bricks were paving in your part of the country and stayed intact, they will work well. You can also find new brick that's been tumbled and splashed with white and black paint to resemble used brick. This type comes with a weather rating.

"Frogged" bricks, stamped with the name of the manufacturer, turn a used-brick walkway into a conversation piece.

Concrete Pavers

Concrete pavers are modular paving units tinted in various colors. The manufacturing process results in concrete that's especially dense and frost-resistant, so pavers are suitable for any climate. Besides being shaped and tinted to resemble brick (see page 13), they come in many other sizes and shapes. Large pavers may be rectangular, round, or hexagonal. They make attractive stepping-stones. Some have an exposed-aggregate surface, while others are fairly smooth. Interlocking concrete pavers are designed to fit together without mortar. They include simple squares and rectangles, as well as intriguing jigsaw-puzzle shapes.

Interlocking concrete pavers in two sizes and a blend of slightly different colors give this patio the look of a European courtyard paved with stone cobblestones.

Concrete cobblestones simulate the look of weathered stone. Manufacturers tumble the pieces to give them rounded edges, and they usually sell a mixture of shades. Cobblestones come in various sizes and shapes, as well as in collections that you can use to create circular or fan-shaped patterns reminiscent of European patios and walkways. Although it's possible to create these patterns with standard rectangular pavers or genuine cobblestones, using the ensembles saves you from cutting numerous pieces. You can also buy concrete cobblestones already attached to nylon mesh in circular, fanned, or straight patterns, which make installation a breeze.

Concrete cobblestones

Concrete pavers

Standard stretcher block

Concrete Blocks

Concrete blocks offer a quick way to build a wall. Standard stretcher blocks typically have two large holes, or cells, that you can leave open or fill with mortar for extra strength. The holes also make it easy to add metal reinforcement where needed. Another type of concrete block interlocks, so you can set the blocks on top of each other to form a firm wall. With either type, you can apply a stucco-like surface-bonding cement to both sides of the wall to give it extra strength (see page 137).

Manufacturers list standard block according to nominal dimensions—8 inches high by 8 inches wide by 16 inches long. Pieces are actually $^3/_8$ inch smaller in each dimension to account for mortar space. They can also be purchased as half blocks, corner pieces, and special shapes for use around windows and doors, which might come in handy for garden walls where you want to add a gate.

Decorative concrete blocks come in many styles. Split-face blocks function like standard stretchers, but they have a textured front. The blocks are made in pairs, then chopped in half with a guillotine, so each piece has a slightly different texture. Screen or grille blocks form patterned walls that admit light and air while providing some privacy. They are only 3 inches thick and must be laid in a single wythe—meaning the wall can be only one block thick—so they should be reinforced with pillars at least every 8 feet.

Grille block

Split-face block

Stackable retaining block

Stackable retaining blocks interlock without mortar to form a wall solid enough to keep a slope or a garden bed firmly in place. The blocks are easy to install and are widely available. They may be rectangular for straight walls or trapezoidal for curves. You don't need a poured foundation, just a gravel base and gravel backfill so any water behind the wall can drain out (see page 122). Once you have excavated for the base, stacking the blocks will likely take only a few hours.

The blocks are designed so that they automatically batter, or slope, the retaining wall the correct amount from one course to the next. Check with your building department, because there may be special rules for even low retaining walls. Also check the manufacturer's specifications. Some styles can be used for walls up to 4 feet high, but height limits vary. If you want to tuck plants into the wall, get blocks that are hollow in the center.

The blocks in this wall are rounded on the front face, giving them a stone-like appearance. Except for the capstones, the top and bottom surfaces of each block are molded with ridges and depressions that interlock. This allows a wall as high as 4 feet if gravity alone holds pieces in place. With engineering and reinforcement, these blocks can rise 30 feet high.

Pigment, sawn lines, and texture applied only to small squares give this concrete patio its distinctive look. The face sculptures are also concrete.

Poured Concrete

Inexpensive and long-lasting, poured concrete is one of the most popular options for patios and walkways. Concrete is a mixture of portland cement, water, and aggregate (usually a combination of sand and gravel, though sometimes only sand or only gravel). Cement, the smallest component, acts like glue to hold the stone bits together.

Color can be added to concrete in several ways. When pigment is mixed into the concrete along with the other ingredients, it's known as integral color. If an edge chips, the underlying concrete blends in. There's no extra labor involved, but you pay for the pigment. Broadcast color is tossed onto and troweled into freshly poured concrete, so the color is only near the surface. You can use several different colors and wind up with interesting mottled effects. It's also possible to combine the two approaches and wind up with concrete that's one basic color throughout but that has streaks or swirls of another color on the surface. A third approach involves applying a decorative stain after the concrete hardens. One kind, known as acid stain, reacts with ingredients in the concrete and permanently changes the color of the material near the surface.

Texture also adds interest to concrete and makes it less slippery. Although it's possible to cut patterns with a grinder or saw after concrete stiffens, textures are easier to create when the mix is still somewhat plastic. You can create a broomed surface, which has a series of straight or curved lines, by dragging bristles across the surface. With a brick jointer or other simple tool, you can outline flagstone shapes and simulate the look of grout lines between stones. And there are stamped designs, created with special textured mats or materials that you improvise. Stencil patterns used in combination with textured rollers are another option.

Exposed aggregate is concrete with pebbles partially embedded on top. Most stones aren't as porous as cement, so this surface resists stains better than standard concrete does. The pebbles also provide better traction. Some people like exposed-aggregate finishes because they are decorative but don't mimic something else. You can opt to expose gravel and sand that are already in the basic concrete mix, or scatter additional pebbles on top. If you want an expensive kind of stone on the surface, broadcasting is more cost-effective because it uses a smaller amount.

Concrete can be tinted and textured to resemble stone paving with either stamps (see pages 106–107) or stencils and textured rollers (see pages 108–109). This patio was stenciled, sprinkled with pigments in several colors, and textured with a roller.

Like bubbles in a bath, circles of concrete appear to float on an expanse of loose gravel in this yard. The large circles feature an exposed-aggregate finish, while the small ones are smooth concrete.

Ceramic Tile

If you're looking for splashes of vibrant color or a patio surface as smooth as the floor of an indoor room, ceramic tile is your best choice. Some types are virtually stain-proof, so you don't have to worry about damage from spilled food or from fruit that drops from nearby trees. However, ask plenty of questions before you buy. Some tiles will crack if they are used outdoors where winters are cold, and some have surfaces that are too soft or too slippery for outdoor paving.

Ceramic tile is made from clay and fired in a kiln. The tiles can be left unglazed, or they can be coated with a baked-on decorative layer. Some glazes have a slightly bumpy surface, which provides skid resistance. High-gloss glazes are generally too slippery.

In most cases, ceramic tile must be set in a bed of mortar (usually thinset mortar) atop a solid concrete slab. You'll also need grout to fill spaces between tiles. Choose a contrasting grout color to emphasize individual tiles, or a grout color that blends in with the tiles to make the paving seem more like one solid piece. Latex-reinforced sanded grout is a good choice for most outdoor applications. Be sure to check labels for recommended joint widths.

TOP: Step risers are a great place to use tile that's too slippery, too susceptible to scratches, or just too bright to be used for a main expanse of paving.

ABOVE: A mosaic of tile and stone adorns this pathway. Glazed tile isn't usually suitable for outdoor paving because it's too slick, but mosaics are an exception. Using small pieces and surrounding them with mortar add the necessary traction.

Porcelain tiles are made from dry-pressed porcelain clay fired at very high temperatures. Porcelain tiles are virtually impervious to water, so they can be used even where winters are cold. They are also incredibly stain-resistant, making them a great choice for outdoor paving where you're worried about spills. Glazed porcelain tiles, like standard glazed ceramic tiles, have a design layer on top of the clay. Through-body porcelain tiles have the same color all the way through, which makes chips or scratches less noticeable. Porcelain tile is often textured and colored to resemble stone or other paving materials.

Mexican saltillos and terra-cotta tiles have a soft reddish glow that lends warmth to a patio (shown at left). However, most types are suitable only for warm climates. With one hard freeze, they could crack. If you like the look but need something more durable, consider porcelain tiles that have a similar appearance.

> **MAINTENANCE TIP**
>
> To keep gravel paving from being tracked inside, buy pieces that are too large to be caught in the treads of shoes. Round pebbles $5/8$ inch in diameter will stay put, and they're more work for cats to dig in.

Loose Materials

Materials such as pebbles, wood chips, and shredded bark offer an easy, economical option for patios and walkways. For a silent path that's easy to walk on, get crushed gravel that includes small particles. If you want a path that crunches underfoot, pea gravel is a great choice. Loose paving needs to be replenished occasionally, as it gets tracked away or breaks down. Home centers typically sell loose materials in bags suitable for small projects. At a stone yard, sand and gravel company, garden center, or building materials supplier, you may find bins of loose materials, which you can shovel into your pickup or have delivered.

Pine needles, which are sold as mulch in some parts of the country, make a path that's as quiet and soft underfoot as a route through deep woods. They will need to be replenished frequently.

Mexican pebbles

San Simeon beach stone

Red lava

White dolomite rock

Crushed granite

Black lava

Navajo rock   Serpentine

Pea gravel

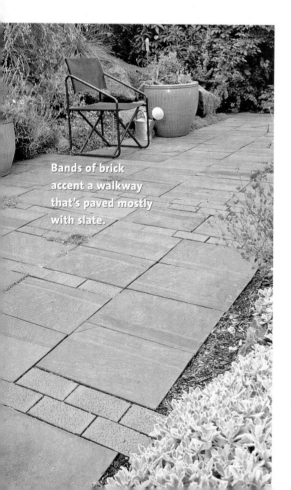

Adobe Block

Traditional adobe block is made from a mix of sand, clay, water, and usually straw. The mixture is placed in molds and allowed to dry in the sun. If blocks become damp, they swell and soften, so true adobe buildings need roofs and exterior plaster. Today, though, you can also buy stabilized adobe, which incorporates cement or asphalt emulsion so that it holds up outdoors, even in wet climates.

Adobe pavers are $2^{1}/_{2}$ inches thick. These are 12 × 12 inches.

Adobe blocks for walls are massive, often 4 × 8 × 16 inches.

Paved with squares of adobe, this dining patio blends in with the surrounding oak-studded hillsides.

Set adobe pavers in sand, not in a mortar bed on concrete. In garden walls, you can leave stabilized adobe blocks exposed or cover them with plaster. Susan Gerome, whose Mule Creek Adobe company in New Mexico makes asphalt-stabilized blocks and pavers, says she's found no damage in pieces left out in the snow in winter or used as steppingstones in a creek for five years.

In the Southwest, where the manufacturers are, adobe pavers may cost less than brick or concrete pavers. Some companies will ship elsewhere, but transportation boosts the price.

Bands of brick accent a walkway that's paved mostly with slate.

Mixed Materials

Paths, patios, and walls of mixed materials catch the eye and invite people to delight in contrasting colors and textures. The contrasts can be bold and bright or quite subdued, depending on your style. Either way, the materials you combine will define your garden as a personal space that reflects your creativity. Selecting materials with colors or textures that are similar usually creates a restful look, while pairing materials with opposite colors or textures results in a livelier look.

A few tricks help keep projects from looking like a jumble of disconnected parts. Just as with plants in a perennial border, mixed materials look better when they are grouped or repeated, not used singly. If you arrange materials in a pattern, for example, repeat it along your wall or path. Or lay out paving in a geometric pattern and fill some spaces with one type of material and others with a contrasting material. For walls, consider using one kind of material as pillars or capstones and another material for the body of the wall. It's best to avoid mortaring dissimilar materials together, however, because they will expand and contract at different rates as moisture and temperature fluctuate.

LEFT: Brick edging and steps embellish the look of this exposed-aggregate path.

RIGHT: A simple gravel path becomes a major design element when other elements, such as a stone grinding wheel and bricks, are introduced. Mortar alone won't hold bricks used like this. They need to sit on concrete and be mortared to it as well.

BELOW: Mosaic tile, smooth-cut stone, and round gravel make an unusual but striking combination, especially when set off by a few purple accents and foliage in many shades of green.

MAKING A PLAN

TAKE TIME TO DREAM A BIT as you begin the design process. In addition to gathering ideas from this book, look at yards in your neighborhood and note materials, structures, and layouts that appeal to you. Paths, patios, and walls play a huge role in shaping how you use outdoor space, so have a family meeting and assess what everyone wants.

Start your planning by thinking of your outdoor living space in terms of defined areas that are joined by paths. A spacious patio works best for sit-down dining, while a small, more isolated patio may be better for contemplation or reading a book. Paths should link areas you use often, such as routes between the front or back door and your parking spaces, compost pile, or vegetable plot. Paths

that draw the eye off into the distance create the illusion of greater space. Walls can signal changes in elevation or use of space, and they're excellent ways to increase privacy or a sense of shelter.

ABOVE: **Even in a modest-size backyard, you may want to create more than one seating area to accommodate a variety of activities. Here, a patio next to the house is perfect for dining and outdoor cooking, while a smaller patio under a trellis roof encourages quiet conversation and relaxation.**

RIGHT: **As you sketch features for your garden, make sure every path has a purpose, even if it's just to carry the eye toward a focal point. This short path focuses attention on the bench and trellis, as well as getting people from the lawn to the seating area.**

RIGHT: **A circular patio 7 feet in diameter has just enough room for a tiny table and two small chairs— perfect for watching birds as you sip morning coffee or for pausing to chat with a friend.**

Well-placed lighting makes an outdoor living space usable at all hours and accents attractive features of your landscape. Make sure any wiring that needs to go underground is in place before you build paths, patios, or walls. If you need an electrical receptacle or want lights that operate on standard current, have an electrician run cable, perhaps through a conduit, and take care not to damage the lines while you excavate or build.

Low-voltage lighting, available in convenient kits, can usually be installed after structures are built, but plan ahead so you won't wish later that you had put part of the system underground. You'll need to plug the adapter into a receptacle and run the thin lines in shallow trenches or staple them to the undersides of structures. The lights themselves can usually be simply poked into the ground or screwed to a wooden or masonry structure.

Lights for paths or security should be controlled by photocells that turn power off in the daytime, or by motion sensors. Lights for a dining or lounging area should be controlled by a standard switch.

Experiment with ideas by sketching on paper, but also test your ideas at full scale. Use a hose, rope, or stakes and twine to mark the outline of a future patio or path. Large cardboard boxes can stand in for garden walls. Then set out the patio furniture—table and chairs, barbecue unit, perhaps lounging furniture—to see how the layout feels.

Defining Areas and Paths

As you define spaces in your yard and lay out paths to connect them, be aware of time-tested rules of thumb for dimensions that work. Don't forget to make room for paths to take people around defined areas. For example, if people will walk by a dining area to get to a barbecue area, you need to leave space for a path where tables and chairs aren't in the way.

A path 4 feet wide is generous, as it allows two people to pass. Paths with less traffic can be 2 or 3 feet wide. Paths where one person goes occasionally, such as to weed perennial beds, can be as little as 18 inches wide.

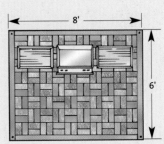

BARBECUE AREA

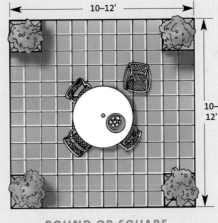

ROUND OR SQUARE TABLE WITH CHAIRS

LOUNGE CHAIR WITH SMALL TABLE

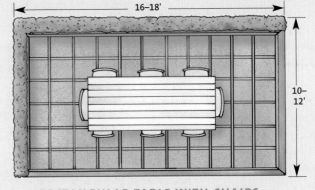

RECTANGULAR TABLE WITH CHAIRS

If you opt to work on paper, basic drafting tools ease the task. A transparent drafting ruler enables you to draw parallel lines that are consistently spaced. For a simple radius curve, use a compass. Use a bendable curved-line tool for more complex curves. Graph paper helps keep features lined up. If you want plans without lines, choose graph paper with blue lines and make a copy of the completed plan after adjusting the copier to a light setting.

DESIGN TIP

Besides creating a base map by measuring everything in your yard, you can also work off of a survey drawing, subdivision plot, or deed for your lot, or from an aerial photograph. You may be able to obtain these through your local assessor's office or planning department, or its web site. Or use an online service. If the map isn't already in a convenient scale, use the enlargement settings on a copy machine to adjust the size.

Mapping Major Features

You can work out ideas with a computer program or on paper. Either way, you'll need to start with an accurate map of your yard or at least the portion you are landscaping. Professionals usually draw landscape plans to a scale of 1 to 10, which means that 1 inch on paper represents 10 feet on the ground. This scale is easy if you use an architect's scale ruler, available at stationery and art-supply stores. With a standard ruler, it's easier to make each inch represent 4, 8, or 16 feet.

Details are important. Show the location of windows and doors, spigots, any utility meters where you must provide access, and any easements. Draw circles to show the approximate canopy of trees, not just the location of their trunks.

When your base map is complete, make several photocopies and sketch the new landscaping features on the copies. If you draw precise details, even down to individual bricks, you can use the drawings to calculate quantities and point out places where your plan creates unnecessary work, such as a patio size for which you'd need to cut bricks along all edges. You can also test your ideas by putting scaled-down patio furniture and large flowerpots on your map.

Besides top-down plan-view maps, also prepare detailed side-view, or elevation, drawings. These show the thickness of various layers, such as gravel and sand, and point out how things are put together.

Find out whether you need a building permit before you finalize your plan and purchase materials. Local governments have different policies about requiring building permits for walks, walls, and patios, and the construction details they may require also differ to account for local weather, soil conditions, wind, earthquake potential, and other factors. Take tentative plans with you when you apply for a permit, and ask whether any of the construction details you show need to be changed. Be sure to ask how any drainage features should be constructed.

If a project does require a permit, you will probably need two inspections, one for the excavation and one for the finished job. Some inspectors have little patience for homeowners—they prefer working with pros. However, if you show you are eager to follow instructions, the relationship will probably be friendly and helpful.

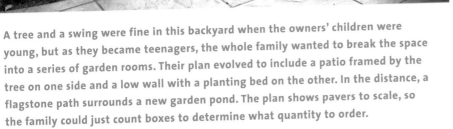

A tree and a swing were fine in this backyard when the owners' children were young, but as they became teenagers, the whole family wanted to break the space into a series of garden rooms. Their plan evolved to include a patio framed by the tree on one side and a low wall with a planting bed on the other. In the distance, a flagstone path surrounds a new garden pond. The plan shows pavers to scale, so the family could just count boxes to determine what quantity to order.

Mapping Trick

A method called triangulation helps you accurately place a feature on a map. Prepare a base map that's exactly to scale and shows at least two fixed spots, such as corners of your house. Then measure from the two fixed points to another feature you want to map. Use a calculator or an online conversion tool to change both measurements to the scale of the drawing. For example, if the scale is 1 inch to 10 feet, divide one distance in feet by 10 to get the number of inches on the map. Set a compass to that distance and draw an arc. Repeat this for the other measurement. The intersection of the arcs marks the location of the feature.

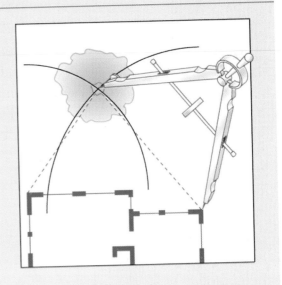

MOVING HEAVY MATERIALS

CALCULATE THE MATERIALS YOU NEED by using dimensions on your completed plan. Suppliers sell most paving and some wall material by the square foot. Sand, gravel, and concrete are sold by the cubic foot if you buy them in bags, and by the cubic yard if you order them in bulk. Suppliers are adept at calculating quantities if you specify the dimensions, so always ask for this help as a double-check on your own figures.

Unless the job is small or you own a heavy-duty truck, it is probably worth the extra expense to have materials delivered to your yard. Discuss details of the delivery when you make the purchase, and take along snapshots of your site if there are special issues. These might include overhead power lines or tree limbs, which could interfere with the operation of a dump truck, or a septic tank, which could be damaged if heavy materials are set on top. Also be aware that a concrete driveway can crack if a truck driver drops a heavy pallet instead of lowering it slowly. A lawn is easier to repair.

Arranging for delivery right next to the job can save you plenty of heavy lifting. A forklift or a skid-steer loader will fit through a 6-foot-wide opening, while miniature excavators and motorized wheelbarrows need as little as 28 inches.

> ## TIME-SAVING TIP
>
> Besides protecting yourself, also protect your lawn if you must move heavy loads over it. Lay a path of 2 × 12s or plywood.

Lifting and Carrying Techniques

Even if you are in good shape, moving wall and paving materials stresses joints and muscles, especially those in the lower back. It's not just the heavy lifting. The repetitive motions also can leave you feeling pain the next morning. So take it easy and minimize lifting whenever possible. When you must do the grunt work, stand up and stretch every few minutes, take plenty of breaks, and get help when necessary.

RIGHT: Keep your feet apart when you lift a heavy object, and hold it close to your body. Holding the item farther away would multiply the force on your lower back.

ABOVE: This motorized wheelbarrow carries a quarter of a ton and fits through gates just 28 inches wide.

A hand truck is a great way to move heavy materials. Ask a helper to tilt the item just enough so you can scoot in the hand truck's base plate. Then tilt the handle back until you feel no pressure on it. Roll the cart along at that angle.

Make a simple ramp from a 2 × 12 with 2 × 2 crosspieces screwed on every 16 inches or so. As you roll materials up the ramp, the crosspieces will keep things from sliding back.

Drag, roll, tip, or pry materials into place whenever possible. Use levers and ramps to move large stones. A rock bar, a thick iron tool with a handle at least 4 feet long, can move even incredibly heavy stones. The longer the handle, the easier the job becomes. For a fulcrum, place a small rock or sturdy piece of wood under the bar close to where it contacts the stone. As you inch the stone along, keep moving the fulcrum. To raise heavy pieces for placement in walls or steps, build a ramp from wood that is nominally 2 inches thick (really 1½ inches).

Lift with your legs and hinge forward at your hips instead of bending your back. This protects your lower back, which is the most susceptible to long-term damage. Wear a lifting belt only if a doctor or therapist has recommended it. Although many people think that lifting belts improve safety, research hasn't found a consistent benefit. Proper lifting technique is better protection.

LABOR-SAVING TIP

If you need to get materials into a backyard but the only way in is through a side gate that's too narrow for the delivery equipment, consider removing a section of fence. Fixing the fence afterward might take a lot less effort than moving materials yourself.

CUTTING TECHNIQUES

SAVE A LOT OF TIME by designing paving or walls to minimize the number of bricks, stones, or blocks you need to cut. If you need to trim only a few pieces, ask the store where you purchased materials to make the cuts for you. Or try using simple hand tools, but practice on scrap pieces first. If you have numerous cuts to make, use tools like those that professionals use. With rentals, you pay by the day. If you need to make cuts over many days, you might save money by buying the tool.

As you decide whether to cut by hand or with a machine, also factor in the degree of precision that you need. Bricklayers usually cut wall bricks by hand because mortar evens out spacing if the bricks wind up slightly the wrong size. But they use machines for paving bricks, which usually need to be cut more precisely. Concrete pavers are virtually impossible to cut by hand.

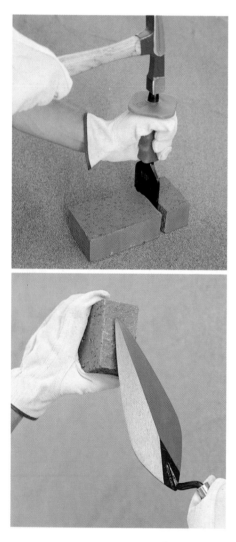

Scoring and Breaking Bricks or Blocks

This is the low-tech way to shape bricks or concrete blocks.

1 **SCORE AND BREAK THE PIECE.** Place the brick or block on a flat, resilient surface, such as a bed of sand. Use a brickset chisel on bricks and a cold chisel on blocks. Press the chisel firmly into place and tap it with a hammer to score a line. Score all four sides of bricks and the top and bottom faces of blocks. Then hold the chisel against the score line, with its bevel (the angled side of the tip) facing the waste side of the cut. Whack the chisel hard with a hammer, and the piece will break.

2 **CLEAN THE CUT EDGE.** Chip or scrape away any protrusions along the cut edge using a brick trowel or a brick hammer.

Using a Brick Splitter

A brick splitter (right) makes fairly accurate cuts without generating dust or much noise, and one can usually be rented for a modest price. Mark the cut line and align it with the splitter's blade. Press the brick snugly against the guide. Push down forcefully on the splitter's handle.

Cutting Flagstone by Hand

Only some types of flagstone can be cut easily by hand with just a tap or two, while others require stronger effort. Score a shallow groove across the stone by tapping with a hammer or on a cold chisel or a stone chaser chisel. It might be enough to score only the top, or you might need to score all four faces. Position the stone so the scored line across the wide face rests over a scrap of wood, a pipe, or another stone slab. Using a small sledgehammer, hit the stone on the waste side to break it off (shown at left).

Using a Power Saw to Cut Materials

The quickest, most foolproof way to cut bricks, stones, or concrete pavers is with a saw or grinder equipped with a diamond blade. An inexpensive abrasive blade works, but a diamond blade cuts faster and smoother. Wet sawing keeps down dust and is much more pleasant than sawing dry. Wear safety goggles.

Use a tabletop wet saw if you are working with bricks or other small pieces with flat sides. For a straight cut, place the brick or other material on the tray and hold it against the back guide so it's square to the blade. Turn on the saw and check that water flows to the blade. Slide the tray forward to slice through the piece.

1 **MAKING ANGLE CUTS.** You'll need a special guide. One type holds pieces at 45 degrees and other specified angles. An adjustable angle guide is also available. Hold the piece firmly against the attachment and slide the table forward to make the cut.

2 **CREATING CUTOUTS.** To notch a piece, make two cuts that result in a notch. Tilt the material up to avoid over-cutting the top. The bottom of the cut will be slightly longer. Hold the piece against the back guide to ensure a square cut.

3 **NIBBLING A CURVE.** Cut a curve by making multiple parallel cuts. Hold the piece firmly with both hands and tilt it up so that the cuts are slightly deeper on the bottom than on the top. Break out the remaining material with a brickset chisel. Clean up the cut by pressing the paver gently against the blade and moving it from side to side. Keep fingers away from the blade.

For larger pieces or situations in which you want to cut materials after they are in place, rent a wet-cutting circular saw, masonry cut-off saw, or grinder.

1 **SCORE A LINE.** Mark the cut line on the front of the stone. If you want a slightly irregular edge, measure the offset and transfer the line to the back of the stone. Barely score the line by lightly going over it with a masonry saw that's running dry. This makes the line easier to see once you turn the water on. Wet-saw along the line in several passes until the cut is deep enough.

2 **SNAP THE PIECES.** With the stone right side up, hit the waste part with a hammer until the stone breaks. Setting the good part on a stiff support, such as a metal bar, makes snapping easier.

3 **CLEAN UP THE EDGE.** To give the ragged edge a worn look, break off some of the protruding sharp pieces with a hammer.

In a pinch, use a standard circular saw (right) or grinder fitted with a diamond blade. To keep down dust, set a fan in front of you and a sprinkler behind so the dust blows into the sprinkler's mist and settles to the ground. Clamp several bricks together to cut them all to the same length. Attach a scrap piece of wood to your work surface to keep the bricks from sliding as you cut.

Measuring for Angle Cuts

On a patio where pavers must be cut precisely, install all the full-size pavers first, then mark the fill-in pieces that need to be cut. This makes it easier to achieve tight fits. If you are renting a saw, it also saves money because it reduces the time you'll need the machine. To ensure that you are getting a consistent angle on individual pieces, double-check your cut mark with a T bevel set to the appropriate angle.

1 **MAKE A MARK.** Mark both sides of the cut, then draw a straight line between the marks.

2 **DOUBLE-CHECK.** To set a T bevel, hold it in place as shown, then tighten the wing nut to preserve the angle.

Marking Border Cuts

When brick or paver paths or patios curve, you're almost certain to wind up with some tiny pieces along the edge. For a neater appearance, install a row of uncut pavers as a border. The best way to do this is to install the main expanse of paving first, then deal with the border. Mark the pieces that need to be cut. Don't measure. That takes too much time and could lead to errors. Instead, trace alongside a full brick or paver, or set pavers at each end and snap a line between them.

walks and

patios

WALKS AND PATIOS RANGE FROM SIMPLE EXPANSES OF GRAVEL,
TO DRY-LAID PAVING WHERE PLANTS GROW BETWEEN PAVERS, TO
SMOOTH EXPANSES OF CONCRETE OR TIDY MORTARED MATERIALS.
THE FOLLOWING PAGES SHOW A WIDE RANGE OF OPTIONS AND
WALK YOU THROUGH THE STEPS NEEDED TO COMPLETE A PROJECT
SUCCESSFULLY.

BUILDING PATHS AND PATIOS

BESIDES DEVELOPING A PLAN AND PURCHASING MATERIALS, preparing for a path or patio involves the key decision of whether to tackle the job yourself or to get professional help. Luckily for you, if you are on a tight budget, some of the materials that are easiest for homeowners to install also tend to cost the least. These include gravel and paving set on a gravel base. Mortared paving, which needs to rest on a concrete base, costs the most. However, if you have an existing concrete path or patio and want to cover it with brick, stone, or tile, the job becomes less costly and more doable. So you'll need to consider all the variables for your specific situation.

ABOVE: Crushed stone from a local quarry gives this patio an informal air that suits the surrounding plants, which include a gnarled California pepper tree, ornamental grasses, and a cactus. Gravel or other loose materials work well for paths or patios that run right up to the base of large trees. Moisture can still reach the roots, and the gravel adjusts as the roots grow, so you don't need to worry about whether the roots will crack or lift the paving.

RIGHT: A flagstone path curves informally as it passes beneath an arbor. To build a path like this, you can either set stones one at a time (see pages 36–37) or install them on a compacted gravel base, as if you were building a patio (see pages 42–43 and 56–57).

LEFT: This vegetable patch looks as elegant and tidy as the most well-tended flower garden, thanks largely to its brick paths with raised wooden edging.

BELOW: Set in mortar, Connecticut bluestone is an ideal paving choice for this patio and pool surround. The stone has a craggy, flamed surface, which provides enough traction to keep wet feet from slipping. And the mortared joints help make the patio easy to keep clean. It can be rinsed or even carefully power-washed when necessary, without the risk of loosening grit between pavers.

ABOVE: A sand-set flagstone walkway transitions to brick and then mortared stone tiles as visitors near this front door, sending a subtle signal that they are leaving outdoor space and entering a family home. There is also a practical reason for the transition: The *Dichondra micrantha* that's flourishing between the flagstones couldn't survive on the covered stoop.

THE SIMPLEST PATH

STEPPINGSTONES ARE THE MINIMALIST APPROACH TO PAVING. They're relatively inexpensive and easy to install without much equipment. And when you're done, the completed path tends to become one with its surroundings. There are trade-offs, of course. While a steppingstone path is good for walking on, it's not great for pushing a wheelbarrow across. And steppingstones require people to think about where to place their feet, so they're often not the best choice for busy traffic routes.

Use a garden hose or two to lay out a pleasing curve for a stepping-stone path. One hose is great for an all-in-a-line walkway. If you arrange steppingstones to match a person's stride, place two hoses about 2 feet apart and keep steppingstones within them.

Design Issues

Before you purchase steppingstones, decide whether you want to set them flush with the soil or elevate them an inch or two. On a manicured lawn, steppingstones will be fully exposed. You can run a lawn mower over them if they are set flush. But if you plan to use a string trimmer, elevating the pieces helps keep you from cutting back too far. If the path traverses a soggy area, elevated stones stay cleaner too. If you plan to surround steppingstones with plants other than a lawn, research the plants' habits and buy stones large enough so that you will still have a usable path after the plants have grown.

Buy steppingstones at least 18 inches wide, 15 to 18 inches deep, and 2 inches thick—or even thicker if you want to elevate them. Steppingstones aren't wedged together, so they need to be thick to remain stable. Options range from flagstones with natural edges to stone tiles and precast concrete steppers in uniform square, octagonal, or round shapes.

Arrange the stones in one of two ways. For a path that's easy to use, place pieces in a subtle zigzag that matches your natural gait. For this, alternate pieces so that one is slightly to the right and the next is slightly to the left. For the other approach, which is especially good for a path designed to carry the eye into the distance, place the pieces in a line. If the steppingstones have irregular shapes, align their centerlines. For a neat look, keep spacing between pieces consistent. With either style, paths usually look best if the longer dimension of the steppingstones runs across the path, not in line with it. Have family members walk on the stones to determine the most comfortable arrangement.

Setting the Stones

You can set steppingstones in soil, but adding a bit of sand makes the installation easier because sand moves to accommodate the stone's shape.

1 **SLICE THE STONE'S OUTLINE.** To mark the outline of a stone that will be set into the lawn, leave the piece in place for a week. When you pick it up, the yellowed grass will show you where to cut. Or set the stone in place and use a shovel to slice a line through the sod around the stone.

2 **REMOVE SOD AND DIG THE HOLE.** Dig up and remove the sod under the stone. Dig out all organic material, including any roots, but don't dig deeper than necessary. Ideally, go just deep enough so that you can add ½ to 1 inch of sand and wind up with the stone at the height you want. If you dig too deep, tamp the soil firm using a 2 × 4, or reduce the risk of future settling by filling the excess space with finely crushed gravel and tamping it firm.

3 **ADD SAND AND BED THE STONE.** Add ½ to 1 inch of damp sand and spread it. If the stone is uneven in thickness, roughly mirror the stone's contours with the sand. Set the stone in place. Tap the stone with a rubber mallet or step on it.

4 **RESHAPE THE SAND AND REPLACE THE STONE.** Lift the stone up to reveal voids and high spots. Scrape the high spots and fill the voids with sand, then replace the stone. Walk on the stone. If it wobbles even slightly, pick it up and add more sand or scrape it where needed.

LAYOUT AND EXCAVATION

MOST PATHS AND PATIOS require more preparation steps than it takes to set steppingstones. To ensure a professional-looking job, you'll need to remove any existing sod or damaged concrete, excavate, install a gravel base, and perhaps add edging and deal with drainage issues. Study the following pages to determine the right sequence for your installation. If you want to preserve existing vegetation along the perimeter, lay out the project before you begin excavating. If you are starting from scratch, it's usually easier to do the careful layout after the gravel base is in place. Install underground wiring, piping, and drainage features that cross under the paving before you add gravel.

Determine the depth of your excavation by adding up the layers of your project. In most cases, you'll need a gravel base at least 4 inches thick in mild climates and at least 6 inches thick where soil freezes. A typical paver installation also calls for 1 inch of sand topped by pavers at least $1\frac{1}{2}$ inches thick. That brings the total excavation to $6\frac{1}{2}$ inches or more. Concrete slabs are usually $3\frac{1}{2}$ to 4 inches thick, with at least that much gravel underneath. However, consult a local contractor or your building department to be sure your installation will be firm enough. Also check whether you need a building permit.

Laying Out a Rectangular Project

When you lay out a rectangular path or patio, it's important to check corners carefully to make sure they are square. If they're off, you could wind up with a project that looks unprofessional. And if you're working with rectangular pavers, you will need to make lots of extra cuts.

Assuming your project extends from a building, drive one nail or pound one stake next to the wall to mark one corner of the paving. Measure along the wall to the next corner and drive another nail or stake. Include the width of any edging in this measurement. Measure out from each corner to determine the approximate location of the final two corners. At each of these, go out about 2 feet on each side and pound a stake or batterboard into the ground. String mason's line (not regular string, which might sag) between these supports to show the tentative perimeter, as shown in the illustration on the opposite page, top. If you are using batterboards, temporarily wrap the lines around them so you can easily move the strings. Or move stakes to reposition the strings.

To check that the corners are square, mark a spot on the building precisely 6 feet from one corner. Wrap tape on the adjacent string precisely 8 feet from the

ABOVE: To lay out a curved corner on a patio that's basic-ally rectangular, first use stakes and mason's line to mark the basic shape with square corners. Tie lines diagonally across the space. Drive a stake along one diagonal, tie a string to the stake, and use a can of spray paint to mark the outline of the curve.

RIGHT: If layout lines are high off the ground, dangle a plumb bob or a chalk line holder from the intersection to mark the exact corner on the ground. Drive a stake there.

corner. Measure the distance between the two marks. If it is precisely 10 feet, the corner is square. If it's not, move the string as needed. For a large patio, increase accuracy by using multiples of 6, 8, and 10, such as 12, 16, and 20. For a path, use 3, 4, and 5. Once one corner is square, measure the diagonals. If they are the same length, all the corners are right. Once you are certain of the lines' positions, mark their locations on the batterboards, or drive stakes deeper.

Making Batterboards

You can use simple stakes to mark a path or patio, but batterboards are sturdier, and they allow you to easily adjust string lines and to remove and later replace them. Pound two 1 × 2 stakes about 18 inches long partway into the ground, then attach a 2-foot-long 1 × 4 horizontally.

Removing Sod

The gravel base of a path or patio needs to rest on undisturbed soil. To make sure you don't dig too far down, excavate in layers. Peeling off any sod is the first step. With hand tools or a machine, you should be able to remove the grass and roots in a fairly uniform layer, without going into the soil underneath. Cut the sod into pieces of manageable weight and roll them up as if they were carpet.

TOP LEFT: A motorized sod cutter makes quick work of large sod-busting jobs. TOP RIGHT: To remove sod with simple hand tools, use a flat spade to cut a line around the perimeter and in parallel lines 18 inches or so apart across the excavation area. Then slice underneath. BOTTOM: A kick-type sod cutter has rollers and a sharp blade that help you slice off a uniform layer.

SAFETY TIP

Before you begin digging, contact your local utility companies to determine the location of any underground wires or pipes.

Demolishing Old Concrete

An old concrete slab that's basically stable can be stained, resurfaced with fresh concrete, or topped with brick, stone, or other paving materials (see pages 66–73). But if the concrete has cracked and shifted in a way that might cause someone to trip, or if it is in the way of a path or patio you want to build, it's time to break out the sledgehammer. Many old patios and sidewalks are only a few inches thick and are relatively easy to break up. Others are thicker and have steel reinforcement, so they require more sweat. Gauge the difficulty by starting in an out-of-the-way corner. Protect your skin and eyes. Whack at the concrete with a sledgehammer. If the slab doesn't crack, remove its support underneath. Poke the tip of a rock bar (a thick steel bar about 6 feet long) a little ways under the concrete, slip a stone or piece of concrete underneath the bar to act as a fulcrum, and press down. When the slab rises, push a rock or a piece of concrete underneath to keep it elevated. Bang again with the sledge. Use lineman's pliers to cut any wire mesh reinforcement. For rebar, use bolt cutters or a hacksaw.

Getting Rid of Sod, Concrete, and Soil

A large trash bin should be the last resort, not an automatic solution, for disposing of the sod, concrete, and soil you remove. You can use chunks of broken concrete like stone to build walls or paving (see pages 72–73 and 128). Sod strips are great for patching lawns or establishing new ones. Use excess soil to fill holes or build up planting beds. If you can't reuse the materials yourself, advertise them in a local paper or online.

Establishing Pavement Height

If you are installing edging that rests directly on soil, you can establish the height of the eventual paving as soon as any sod or unwanted concrete is out of the way. Otherwise, delay this step until the gravel base is installed (see pages 42–43).

In most cases, install paving slightly higher than surrounding soil so you can sweep off debris. If a path crosses a lawn, though, you might prefer paving that's even with the top of the soil so you can mow over the edge.

Paving must slope so rainwater can drain. Paths might need just ⅛ inch of slope per foot, along either their length or their width. For the gentlest slope, create a crown in the center of the path so water drains to both sides. Patios, especially next to a house, need to slope ¼ inch per foot, down and away from the house, though they should be level along the edge parallel to the house. Even patios with sand between joints need to slope.

PROBLEM-SOLVING TIP

If you are building a path or patio that leads off from a doorway or an existing set of stairs, start establishing the height of the new paving there. At stairs, the top of the paving must be at a height that keeps the final step the same height as the others. At a doorway, you will probably want the paving to begin just under the threshold.

1 ESTABLISH A LEVEL LINE. Pound a stake into the ground at each corner where layout lines intersect. If the paving will be next to a building, draw a line on the wall to show the top of the paving. If it will be freestanding, mark one stake instead. Then mark the same height on stakes at the other corners. Use a level strapped to a long, straight board. If a board won't reach across the area to be paved, use mason's line and a line level, a little tool that clips over twine. Establish the level line from your starting point to both adjacent corners and then from one of those to the final corner. Check to make sure lines on the final stake and its other adjacent stake are level.

2 ESTABLISH THE SLOPE. Calculate how much slope you need by multiplying the distance in feet by 0.13 (the rounded-off equivalent of ⅛) or 0.25 (for ¼). For example, a patio 8 feet wide that slopes ¼ inch per foot drops off 2 inches ($8 \times .25 = 2$). On the downward stakes, make a second mark this distance below the level line.

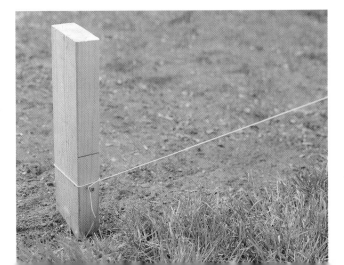

LABOR-SAVING TIP

If you have a large area to excavate, and can't bring in excavating
equipment, consider running a
rototiller over the area after you
have removed the sod. This breaks
up the soil near the surface and
makes it easier to remove.

Preparing the Base

Before you begin excavating for the main expanse of the paving,
investigate whether the job can be done at reasonable cost by
someone with a small earth-moving machine. If so, it usually
makes sense to excavate and add gravel first, then deal with edging.
If you are excavating by hand, you might want to install the finished edging (see pages 46–53) or temporary 2 × 4s staked to the
height of the paving. Then you can measure down from the top to
determine how deep to dig. For wide areas, stretch a grid of taut
mason's line between the edging every 4 to 5 feet and measure down from them.

For the gravel base, order compactible gravel (also known as aggregate base course or
hardcore), made to serve as a patio substrate. This gravel has the right mix of large and
small particles so it will compact well and allow water to drain. To figure how much you
need in cubic yards, see page 88. If possible, have the supplier dump the gravel, or at
least the first layer of it, directly into the hole. Rent a vibrating plate compactor an hour
or two before the gravel will be delivered, so that you can power-tamp the soil first. If
the area is too small to use a vibrating plate compactor, use a hand tamper instead.

1 **EXCAVATING TO DEPTH.** Remove all organic material, including roots, or the paving could buckle in
time. (If you encounter thick tree roots, ask an arborist
whether you can sever them without endangering the health
of the tree; you might need to reevaluate your landscaping
plan.) If you accidentally loosen too much soil, remove it and
replace it with gravel, which compacts better. Dig first with
a pointed shovel, then clean up the bottom of the excavation
with a flat shovel. Its blade may be the correct length to use
as a depth guide. If it's not, mark the depth with tape on the
blade or handle so you can quickly check as you work.

2 **ADDING AND DAMPENING GRAVEL.** Remove
the guidelines and go over the surface four or five
times with the plate compactor. Work in a circular pattern
and overlap passes so you're certain to cover the entire
area. Then add geotextile material, also known as landscaping cloth, if you are using it. Over that, add 4 to 6 inches of
gravel, the depth that compacts well in one pass. Spread it
with a shovel, then rake it. If the gravel is dry, spray it with
water from a hose until it is damp enough that you can
clump it into a ball but not so wet that it drips.

3 **COMPACTING THE GRAVEL.** When you think you are close to the right level, reinstall the guidelines and check for depth. Remove gravel if the level is more than $1/2$ inch too high; tamping will lower the depth by about that much. Then remove the lines, power-tamp several times for firmness, and recheck the depth. Spread more gravel, if needed, and repeat the steps.

Should You Use Landscaping Cloth?

Many people use landscaping cloth—also known as filter fabric, weed cloth, or geotextile—as one layer in a paving project. Spread over an excavation and topped with gravel, it keeps stones from sinking into soggy clay soil. In this application, the fabric should extend up the sides of the hole.

> If you use landscaping fabric, choose heavy material and eliminate folds as you spread it. Overlap parallel strips by 6 to 8 inches.

Some installers use the fabric between gravel and sand layers to keep fine particles from sinking into the gravel, which would plug the gaps needed for water to drain. In this case, the fabric edge should butt tightly against the edging.

One thing landscaping cloth doesn't do is guarantee an absence of weeds in gaps between paving pieces. The cloth does block sprouts and runners that might come up from below, but it does not keep seeds that land on the surface from sprouting and sometimes growing into the cloth, where the weeds are harder to remove.

Dealing with Drainage

If your site has had no discernable drainage problems and the paving will be no wider than 16 feet, you may have no need for drainage measures, other than a slope. However, be aware that unless a patio has wide sand-filled joints between pavers, or you're using pervious paving (see pages 74–75), most rainwater will flow in the direction of the slope rather than into the base of the paving. The larger the patio, the more runoff there will be. You may need to add a drainage system to keep puddles from developing along the edge.

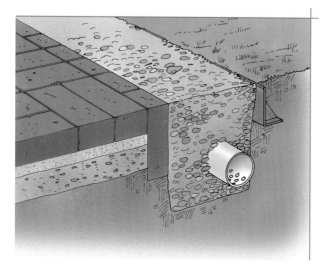

A perimeter trench drains best if gravel particles are all about the same size. To keep the spaces between pieces from plugging up, line the trench with landscaping fabric if your soil has a lot of clay.

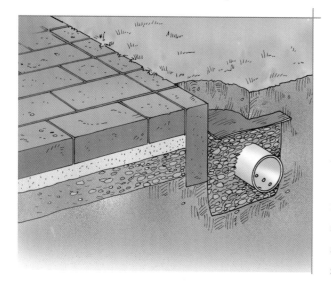

If you want to see lawn next to your paving, put landscaping fabric over the gravel to block silt, then add soil and sod.

A gravel-filled trench at the downhill edge will handle an average puddle problem. Either before or after constructing the patio, dig a 12-inch-deep trench and fill it with decorative gravel or pebbles. If you don't like the look of gravel, dig the trench 16 inches deep and fill all but the top 4 inches with pebbles or stones. Place a layer of landscaping fabric over the gravel, fill the rest of the trench with soil, and plant grass on top. Either way, use rounded gravel, which allows for easy drainage, not compactible gravel.

For greater drainage, lay a perforated drainpipe in the trench, with the holes pointed down so gravel won't clog them. Slope the pipe so it carries water away from the area during a severe rain. Extend the pipe into a planting bed and let the water trickle out there, through the perforations. Or dig a trench and extend the pipe to a point where the water can flow down a hillside or into a dry well or rain garden. Line the trench with landscaping cloth and put in a couple of inches of gravel before you add the pipe. Cover it with more gravel, then wrap the landscaping cloth over that and fill the rest of the trench with soil. If you don't want water to trickle out on the way to the end point, use pipe that's not perforated. Just bury it in soil, without the gravel surround. Regardless of the pipe you use, slope it at least $1/4$ inch per foot. Do not divert water onto someone else's property or release it near the foundation of a building. Contractors with knowledge of local soil conditions and the right equipment can install drainpipe quickly and neatly.

Install a catch basin if you want water to drain into a specific spot rather than along an edge. Slope the paving so the catch basin is at the lowest point. On large patios, that's often the center. Options for disposing of the water are the same as for a gravel-filled trench. Set the grate so it's level with the top of the pavement.

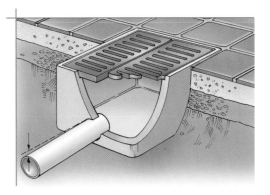

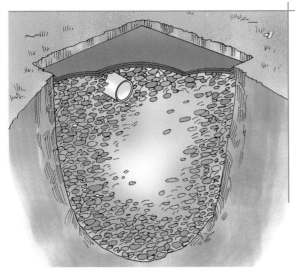

A dry well is simply a large hole filled with rounded gravel. The spaces between pieces act as a reservoir so runoff water can flow in through a pipe during a heavy storm, then slowly percolate into the surrounding soil. Fill a dry well with rounded gravel that has pieces all about the same size. A mixture that includes fine particles doesn't hold as much water, because they fill many of the spaces. A soil engineer can help determine the proper size for the hole, which varies depending on the amount of paving, typical storms in your area, and your soil type. A dry well about 3 feet wide and 3 feet deep will hold a good deal of water. Line the hole with landscaping cloth before you add the gravel. Stop when the hole is not quite full. Add three layers of roofing felt (tar paper), a layer of soil, and sod.

A rain garden serves the same purpose as a dry well, but instead of hiding the storm runoff, the garden turns the water into an amenity. Away from your house, dig a shallow depression in soil and install piping that carries runoff to it. Work a significant amount of compost into the soil, if possible, then plant shrubs or perennials that can withstand having their feet wet periodically. Native species that thrive in flood plains and provide food and cover for birds work particularly well. During a storm, water will flow into the rain garden and puddle, then slowly percolate into the soil.

Soil conditions affect how large the rain garden must be. If puddles persist, enlarge the garden.

RAIN GARDEN

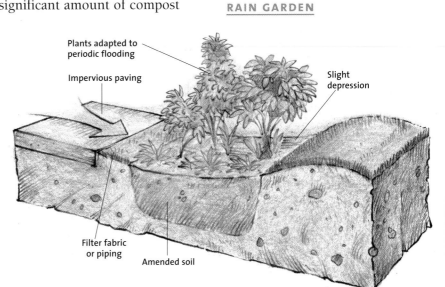

Plants adapted to periodic flooding

Impervious paving

Slight depression

Filter fabric or piping

Amended soil

INSTALLING EDGING

EDGING IS MORE THAN A DECORATIVE BAND around paving. In many cases, it keeps pieces from drifting apart. If you're using large flagstones or cut stone slabs 2 feet square, you don't need edging, as the pieces are heavy enough to stay put. You can also skip edging on concrete slabs or on paths or patios where you are setting bricks or stones in a mortar bed over concrete. But for sand-set brick, concrete pavers, or small pieces of stone, edging is essential if you want pieces to stay aligned.

The base of invisible edging usually points out. However, some edging can be faced inward, allowing you to cover it with the border pavers. This creates a smooth edge that doesn't interfere with landscaping. If you are installing invisible edging with a base that will be covered by pavers, use a few pieces of pavers as spacers and drive the stakes. Then add the rest of the pavers.

Invisible Edging

Plastic and metal edgings hold paving securely in place without drawing attention to themselves. Once backfilled, they can be completely hidden.

These edgings go on top of the compacted gravel base, which must extend beyond the pavers by 6 to 8 inches, depending on the edging manufacturer's specifications. Although you can install the edging and then add bedding sand and pavers, it's often easier to put in the edging after the pavers are in place. Carefully scrape away any bedding sand that extends beyond them so the edging rests on gravel. The edging must be in place before you go over the pavers with a vibrating plate compactor (see page 43).

Plastic and metal edgings usually have an **L** shape when viewed from the end. Snug the vertical part to the pavers and anchor the bottom to the gravel by driving spikes of the recommended length—often 8 to 12 inches—through the perforations. Along straight runs, drive stakes every foot or so—more often if the ground is soft and the spikes are easy to drive. At a curve, drive a spike into every available hole.

Many "landscaping" edgings are designed only to hold back mulch; they are not strong enough for a patio. For true paver edging, look for thick plastic or metal, which is sold at masonry supply companies.

TIME-SAVING TIP

If you are installing paving that comes in set sizes, such as bricks or concrete pavers, you may be able to avoid cutting many pieces if you start with edging installed on only two adjoining sides. Place all the pavers, then snug the final sections of edging up to the outermost pieces.

Wood Edging

Wood edging is made from 2 × 4 or 2 × 6 boards that are straight and free of large knots. Use pressure-treated wood rated for ground contact or a plastic-wood composite. Cedar was once recommended, but most of the second-growth material available today isn't durable enough for permanent edging. If possible, buy pieces long enough for each edge. If you must butt pieces, nail or screw a splice about 2 feet long to the outside edge of both boards. Use material nominally 1 or 2 inches thick for this. Support the edging with stakes every 2 feet or so.

Cut sod back 2 inches from the outside of the edging to make room for the stakes. Excavate deep enough to place at least 2 to 3 inches of rough gravel or pebbles under the boards.

1 **SET THE BOARDS IN PLACE.** Cut the boards to length and set them in place, resting them on gravel at either end. Check the guide strings and use a level to make sure the boards are at the right height and are either level or correctly sloped. You may need to shift gravel or tap a board down. Sight along each board to make sure it is straight.

2 **DRIVE STAKES.** Cut stakes from pressure-treated 2 × 4s. The pointed tips should be about 4 inches long. The length of the stakes depends on soil conditions; it should take some effort to drive them to the desired depth. Hammer against a 2 × 4 scrap, as shown, to prevent the stakes from splitting. Drive stakes about 1½ inches below the tops of the edging boards, or trim them with a handsaw to that length. If the soil is very hard, or if the wood stakes tend to move the edging out of alignment, consider using metal stakes instead.

3 **DRIVE SCREWS AND BACKFILL.** Check again that the edging is correctly aligned. From inside the excavation, drive two 2½-inch deck screws into each stake. Shovel gravel under the edging to support it at all points. (This will prevent the wood from soaking in standing water.) Backfill on the outside of the edging with soil and lightly tamp with a 2 × 4, taking care not to nudge the edging out of alignment. After the patio is laid, tamp soil along the edging more firmly.

Curved wood edging blends in nicely with the gravel surface on this path, and one piece of timber edging serves as a step that converts the sloped route to a couple of flat terraces. Without the step, gravel in the higher area would tend to migrate toward the lower area.

Curved Wood Edging

Form curved wood edging from redwood benderboard, which is about $^3/_8$ inch thick, or thin composite lumber, which is made from plastic and wood fibers. If the curved edging connects with straight edging made of 2 × 4s or 2 × 6s, use several layers of material that bends so that you maintain a consistent thickness at the top edge.

Because it is difficult to accurately measure the length of a curve, especially when multiple layers of a material are involved, it's best to install pieces that are longer than you need and cut them to length after they are in place.

1 **BEND THE BOARDS INTO POSITION.** At the beginning and end of the current run, drive stakes just beyond where the benderboard will be. Trim stakes, if necessary, so tops are $1^1/_2$ inches below the top of the edging. Place the benderboard along the inside edge of one stake, then screw through the benderboard into the stake. Bend the boards to the desired shape and screw them to the other stake. Drive temporary stakes on the inside to hold the edging in place.

2 **INSTALL PERMANENT STAKES.** Use a carpenter's level to check that the edging is level or correctly sloped. Every 2 feet, drive a permanent stake on the outside so that its top is $1^1/_2$ inches below the top of the edging. Drill pilot holes and drive deck screws to attach the benderboards to the permanent stakes. Remove the temporary stakes.

3 **CUT THE ENDS.** At the point where the curve ends and a straight line begins, use a small square to draw a cutoff line. Cut the curved edging with a handsaw or a reciprocating saw.

Timber Edging

Pressure-treated 4 × 4, 4 × 6, or 6 × 6 lumber rated for ground contact creates sturdy edging and and turns an attractive gray in a year or two. Take care to select timbers that are straight, as there is no way to unbend them. Excavate deep enough to accommodate several inches of gravel under the timbers.

1 **CUT AND POSITION THE TIMBERS.** To cut a 4 × 4 or a 4 × 6, use a small square to draw lines around all four sides. Set the blade of a 7¼-inch circular saw to full depth and check that it is square to the saw's base. Cut the two opposite sides of the timber. Cut a 6 × 6 on all four sides, then cut the middle with a handsaw or a reciprocating saw. Treat the cut ends (see tip). Set the timbers in a bed of gravel and check for the correct height and alignment. You may need to remove the timber, add or shovel away some gravel, and try again.

2 **DRILL HOLES.** Anchor the timbers with ½-inch-diameter concrete reinforcement bar (rebar) or ½-inch-diameter galvanized pipe. Equip a drill with an extra-long spade bit that's as wide as the anchors you will use. Drill holes through the center of the timber every 2 feet or so. If the drill or bit starts to get hot, give it a rest.

3 **DRIVE ANCHORS.** Use a hacksaw or a reciprocating saw equipped with a metal-cutting blade to cut lengths of rebar or pipe to 2 feet. Use a sledgehammer to pound each anchor down through the timber and into the ground until the top of the metal is flush with the timber. If you can't drive the spikes all the way in, cut shorter pieces.

Upright Paver Edging

Upright bricks, cobblestones, or concrete pavers make wonderful edging. They can match material used on the rest of a path or patio or provide a pleasant contrast to a different kind of paving. For example, brick paving looks great with cobblestone edging.

No stakes hold this edging in place. Rather, it depends on having undisturbed soil on the outside edge. If your soil is sandy or soft, consider installing paver-on-concrete edging instead (see page 53). Or set the edging in several inches of mortar, as shown on the opposite page. Install upright paver edging before or after you put in the gravel base.

When bricks or other pieces stand upright with a thin edge facing the patio or path, they're called soldiers. Sailors face the other way, as if to catch the wind. Soldiers make stronger edging, but sailors require fewer pieces, so the installation speeds along.

1 **DIG AND SCREED THE BASE.** Stretch a guide string at the level of the patio surface. Dig a trench 4 inches deeper than the height of the pavers. Shovel in 3 inches of gravel and tamp it firm with a hand tamper or with a piece of 4 × 4. Make a screed guide, as shown, from a 2 × 6 and a 2 × 4. The 2 × 6 should extend below the 2 × 4 by the depth of an edging piece. Pour about 1 inch of damp sand over the gravel. Scrape across the sand with the guide. Then spray the sand with a fine mist of water, add a little more sand, and screed again.

2 **SET THE PAVERS.** Position each paver so its outside corner is about ⅛ inch inside the guideline. After you have installed 4 feet or so, lay a straight board on top and tap it to achieve a smooth, even surface.

3 **FILL AND TAMP.** Use a 2 × 4 to gently tamp soil or gravel on the patio side of the edging. If pieces go out of alignment, nudge them back toward the patio side by tamping soil into the space between the sod and the soldiers.

4 **TURNING A CURVE.** To turn a curve, install benderboard edging (page 48) as a guide. Joints between the bricks or other material will be wider on the outside of the curve.

Masonry Edging with Gravel Infill

If you're using masonry edging for a gravel path or patio, you can skip a few steps by following a slightly different procedure.

1 **PREPARE THE HOLE.** Excavate just deep enough so the edging will be 1 inch higher than the surrounding soil. Dig straight down along the edges so you don't disturb the soil beyond.

2 **PLACE THE EDGING.** Line the excavation with landscaping cloth, if you are using it, then place the edging pieces in position.

3 **ADD GRAVEL AND TAMP.** Fill half the excavation with gravel, shovel and rake it level, and mist it with water. Tamp it thoroughly using a hand tamper or a vibrating plate compactor. Then fill the rest of the excavation and repeat. The compacted gravel should wind up slightly lower than the edging.

Tilted Brick Edging

To keep bricks aligned, place them so one top corner is flush with the top of the wooden guide.

This edging adds charm to a patio. Orienting the wide face toward the paving and tilting the pieces will reduce the stability, but there are a couple of ways to add strength. If you live where winters are mild, set the angled bricks in mortar, as shown. If you live where winters freeze, pack mortar or concrete along the outside edge of the bricks instead so any cracks that develop as the soil freezes and thaws won't push the paving out of alignment.

Tilted brick edging usually extends a little higher than the paving it encloses. If you're worried about creating an elevated edge where people might trip, set the uppermost corners of the bricks at the same height as the paving. To install the edging, temporarily stake a wooden guide along the outer edge at the height that you want for the tips, then check that it is level or correctly sloped. Dig a trench 4 inches deeper than the edging pieces will extend downward. Working in sections 3 to 4 feet at a time, shovel a little mortar into the trench and place the bricks tilted at the desired angle.

Poured Concrete Edging

This is the strongest edging. In mild climates, pour the concrete directly on undisturbed soil or on compacted gravel. Where winters are cold, always provide the gravel. To dress up the concrete, tint it or give it a decorative finish as it stiffens (see pages 104–111). Or cover the concrete with tile, flagstone, or brick.

For basic instructions on building forms, mixing concrete, and finishing, see Chapter 3. For crack resistance, this edging should be at least 6 inches wide and 4 inches deep, and there should be a joint every 10 feet. If you will cover the edging with tiles or pavers, make the edging an appropriate width and height to accommodate them.

1 **BUILD THE FORMS.** Dig a trench wide enough for the edging and form boards. Shovel 3 inches of compactible gravel at the bottom and pack it firm with a 2 × 4, 4 × 4, or hand tamper. Build straight forms using 2 × 4s attached to 1 × 2 or 2 × 2 stakes, or build curved forms using benderboard, as shown on page 48.

Check that the forms are at the right height and are either level or correctly sloped. For extra stiffness, you can place lengths of ³⁄₈-inch rebar down the middle of the form. Elevate the metal on rebar bolsters or chunks of stone.

2 **POUR AND SCREED THE CONCRETE.** If the concrete will remain exposed, prepare high-early-strength or fiber-reinforced concrete, both of which are easier to finish than low-priced concrete. (It's fine for concrete that will be topped by pavers, though.) Shovel the concrete into the forms. Poke with rebar along the forms and tap the wood with a hammer to work out air bubbles. Screed, or roughly level, the top by scraping it in a sawing motion with a scrap of lumber.

3 **TROWEL THE TOP.** Wait until water on the surface disappears (usually in about an hour). Smooth the top with a magnesium or wood float. If the concrete will stay exposed, round over the corners with an edging tool and carefully remove the forms on the outside edge once the concrete stiffens (maybe in another hour or two). Then you can smooth over any gaps with a trowel. For a finished appearance, work the surface with a steel trowel or brush it with a broom. Keep the concrete moist for at least several days by covering it with plastic and/or spraying it with water regularly.

Topping Concrete Edging

Bricks, pavers, tiles, and even stones with at least one relatively flat face can be laid on or in concrete edging. See pages 66–67 for a more detailed discussion about mortaring paving to concrete.

To mortar edging onto cured concrete, pour concrete so it's lower than the path or patio by the thickness of the top edging plus about ⅜ inch. Let the concrete cure at least one day. Set the edging pieces on the concrete in a dry run with uniform gaps about ⅜ inch wide. Make any necessary cuts, then move the pieces aside. If the concrete is dry, dampen it or brush on concrete bonding adhesive. Prepare a bag of mortar mix as directed on the package, or substitute bonding adhesive for some of the mix water for greater weather resistance. Spread mortar over several square feet of the edging and set the edging pieces in place. When you finish the section, place a board over the edging and tap down to seat the pieces evenly. After the mortar sets, fill joints with freshly prepared mortar, as shown on page 67.

To set edging directly in poured concrete, build the form using 2 × 6s and make it just wide enough to accommodate the edging. On the inside of each form board, snap a chalk line to show the edging's thickness, minus ½ inch. Mix concrete and pour it into the form almost up to the chalk line. Roughly level the concrete with a scrap of wood. Set pavers in the wet concrete so their tops are barely above the form. Use spacers to keep them about ⅜ inch apart. Work quickly. When you finish a section, tap the pieces flush with the top of the form boards, or place a board over several pieces and tap on that. After the concrete stiffens, fill the joints with mortar.

GRAVEL PATH OR PATIO

GRAVEL IS THE EASIEST PAVING TO INSTALL, and it results in an informal look that's perfect for many situations. Because it allows rainwater to percolate into the soil, it's the ideal paving next to an established tree.

However, there are certain issues you should take into consideration. Gravel stays put only on relatively flat stretches. If you are building a path that slopes, choose another paving material or break the path into terraces separated by steps. Also, you will need to rake regularly if you want to keep the gravel free of needles and leaves, which become a growing medium for weeds if left to decay.

To minimize the chance that gravel will catch on shoes and be tracked indoors, provide at least a short stretch of a different kind of paving near doors. That way, the gravel has a chance to drop off. As an alternative, use round gravel ⅝ inch in diameter, which is too big to lodge in shoe treads. The downside of this is that round gravel doesn't pack as firmly, so it's more difficult to traverse. To overcome this somewhat, use crushed gravel on the bottom and then top it with only a couple of inches of the round material.

Excavate to a depth of 4 to 8 inches, depending on soil and drainage. The deeper end of that range allows more base gravel, which is useful if you have clay soil and poor drainage. Install edging before or after you add the gravel.

MAINTENANCE TIP

A surface made with tiny stones, such as crushed rock or decomposed granite, becomes surprisingly hard once compacted, and puddles can develop in low spots. If you think this may occur, excavate about 8 inches deep and fill the bottom of the excavation with ¾-inch gravel that doesn't contain fine particles. Place landscaping fabric over that, then top it with the smaller gravel.

Gravel makes a good paving choice for garden paths surrounded by raised planters or planting beds. Besides being inexpensive and easy to install, it allows rainwater to percolate through, which encourages plants to develop deeper roots.

Adding a Stabilizer

If you're worried that gravel might migrate into your house, or if you want to keep cats from digging in it, consider spraying the paving with an acrylic or vinyl acetate soil stabilizer. This material binds the gravel to the path and stiffens the surface. It won't work on rounded gravel; you must use crushed gravel that includes fine particles. Gravel ¼ inch or smaller works best, but you can use pieces up to ¾ inch.

Stabilized gravel sheds water, so deal with drainage as if the paving were solid. The material also leaves the path looking a little like it's coated with plastic, so test first to make sure it's what you want.

1 **LAY A GRAVEL BASE.** Shovel and rake a layer of compactible gravel and spray it with a fine mist until it is moist. The thickness of the first layer depends on how you plan to compact the gravel and whether you are using different gravel on top. A vibrating plate compactor can tamp a layer 4 to 6 inches thick, while a drum roller or hand tamper works on half that. If you are using two kinds of gravel, allow at least 2 inches for the top layer.

2 **COMPRESS THE BASE.** If you are building a patio, compress the base gravel with a vibrating plate compactor. If you are building a narrow path, a drum roller may be easier to use.

3 **SPREAD AND RAKE THE TOP COAT.** Use a rake to spread the finish material, taking care not to disturb the base coat. If the material is small-grained, tamp it. Do not attempt to tamp large, rounded pebbles or stones.

Adding Steppingstones to a Gravel Path

To make a gravel path easier to walk on or to cut down on grit that's tracked into a house, add flagstones or other steppingstones and space them to match your stride. Although you can add them to an existing path, they're easier to install as part of the initial construction. Excavate, install edging, and lay a bed of well-tamped gravel that's a steppingstone's thickness below the top of the edging. To set each stone, first pour a small amount of rough sand on the gravel, then work the stone onto the sand so that it does not wobble (see page 37). Once the stones are all in place, use a rake to spread more gravel around the stones, to within ½ inch of the top of the edging. Spray with a mist of water and spread more gravel if needed.

BUILDING WITH FLAGSTONES

IN SOME WAYS, FLAGSTONE PAVING IS A GROWN-UP VERSION of a steppingstone path. But instead of marching as individuals, the stones work as a team. From a construction standpoint, this means that instead of excavating for each individual stone, you prepare a crushed-gravel base that all stones share. Follow the procedure shown on pages 54–55, but use slightly finer crushed gravel at least near the top. It should have particles that range from $\frac{1}{4}$ inch in diameter down to dust. You don't need a leveling layer of sand over the gravel, as you would with bricks or other pavers, because flagstones vary in thickness. You need to adjust each one in order to create a top surface that's as smooth as possible.

For the easiest installation, choose flagstones that are fairly consistent in thickness. A stone yard may allow you to handpick flagstones for a small path or patio, but for a surface larger than 100 square feet, you may need to buy a pallet of stones. Order stone at least $1\frac{1}{2}$ inches thick.

1 **SORT THE STONES.** Move flagstones close to the edge of the area where you are working. As you move them, separate out pieces with a long, straight edge so you can use them along the perimeter. Store especially large slabs on edge to reduce their chances of breaking.

2 **SET THE FIRST PIECES.** If the paving starts at the house, begin by choosing a large flagstone with at least one straight edge for the spot by the door. Set it on the crushed gravel base, but don't attempt to level it yet. If you have a few other especially large slabs, place them randomly across the paving.

3 **FILL AND CUT AS NEEDED.** Working in an area of about 10 square feet, find pieces that fit with little or no cutting. It's like putting a jigsaw puzzle together. Focus on the shape of an empty spot, then look for a piece that matches. Aim to achieve joints that are about 1 inch wide. If you need to trim a stone to get a good fit, set the piece you want to cut on the gravel and overlap it with the adjoining piece. With the tip of a sharp tool, trace against the top stone and scratch a line in the bottom stone where it needs to be cut. Use one of the methods shown on pages 28–31 to make the cut.

4 **SET THE FLAGSTONES.** Once you've settled on stones for the area, set them before you move on to the next area. Start with the stone next to the door, because the height there determines the finished height of your patio. To set a stone, scrape away or add gravel as needed to bring the top surface to the right height. Lift and lower the stones into place; scooting them would push gravel to the side. Even pros often need to lift stones and adjust the base several times to get a good fit. If an edge is just a little too low, lift it with a cat's paw and dribble a little more gravel into the joint. Work the material under the stone with the tool. Later, when you tamp the paving, the cavity will fill in more.

5 **CHECK THE SLOPE.** Every time you set a stone, check with a straightedge to make sure that the top is even with surrounding stones. Using a level as a straightedge also allows you to check that the overall surface slopes in the desired direction. It should slant gently away from the building but be level next to the wall. Make minor adjustments by tamping high stones down with a rubber mallet. Raise low edges as shown in step 4.

6 **FILL THE JOINTS.** Pour sand or fine gravel over the flagstones and use a wide push brush to work the material into the joints. Sweep in several directions until all the voids are filled.

7 **TAMP.** To seat the stones evenly, set plywood or oriented-strand board over a section of the paving. Run a plate compactor over that. Move the wood and repeat on remaining areas.

BRICK OR PAVER PATH OR PATIO

BRICKS, COBBLESTONES, SAWN STONE PAVERS, AND CONCRETE PAVERS can all be installed in a similar fashion. You don't need to fuss about making each piece level. That happens automatically when you use a vibrating plate compactor at the end.

Preliminary steps include excavating, adding a gravel base, and tamping that firm, as shown on the previous pages.

Screeding for Paving with Solid Edges

If you are using wood or another solid edging, proceed as shown here. Then spread bedding sand, also known as underlayment. Particles must be coarse, with none larger than $3/16$ inch.

1 **PREPARE THE SITE.** If you are using landscaping fabric (see page 43), spread it smoothly across the gravel base. If your paving is more than 10 feet wide, install a temporary screed guide by cutting a 2 × 4 to fit 6 to 10 feet away from one edge. Stake the guide so that its top is exactly level with the edging it runs parallel to, then drive the stakes below the top of the guide.

2 **MAKE A SCREED.** Start with a straight 2 × 4 or 2 × 6 that is about 2 feet longer than the area to be screeded. Cut one or more strips of plywood to the thickness of the pavers plus the width of the 2 × 4 or 2 × 6. The plywood should be about 4 inches shorter than the distance you are screeding. Attach the plywood with screws so it extends below the board by the thickness of a paver. If you want pavers to wind up $1/4$ inch higher than the edging, adjust the spacing accordingly.

3 **SPREAD SAND.** Without disturbing the landscaping fabric or the gravel, spread the sand with a square shovel and rake it until it is slightly higher than its final level. The sand should be dry.

4 **SCREED THE SAND.** If the screed is longer than 6 feet, do this step with a helper. Starting at one end, move the screed across the patio to smooth the sand. Fill any voids and repeat until you achieve a perfectly smooth surface.

Using Screed Pipes

Instead of making a screed board and running it across solid edging, you can use pipes as guides for pouring a uniform layer of sand. This method works even for paving that's wider than a screed board can reach and for jobs in which you install part or all of the edging after the paving is placed. Professionals often use electrical conduit as guides, but plastic pipe also works and is inexpensive. For a 1-inch-thick layer of sand, use ¾-inch plastic pipe, which has an outside diameter of about 1 inch. For a 1½-inch-thick layer, use 1-inch pipe.

1 **LAY AND CHECK SCREED PIPES.** Set two or three pipes about 6 feet apart on the compacted gravel base. Lay a straight 2 × 4 across them and check with a level to make sure they have the slope you want on the finished paving.

2 **SPREAD BEDDING SAND.** Pour bedding sand into the area and roughly smooth it with a garden rake so it's slightly higher than the pipes at most points.

3 **SCREED THE SAND.** Lay a straight 2 × 4 across two or three of the pipes. Press the board onto the pipes and pull or push it across the patio to produce a smooth surface. Fill in any low spots and repeat.

4 **REMOVE THE PIPES.** Carefully pick up the pipes and remove them without disturbing the surface. Fill in the voids with sand. Don't worry about making these areas perfectly smooth. You can do that with a trowel later as you place pavers.

Patterns for sand-set bricks are based on an assumption that you're using standard-size pieces, not modular ones that have been cast a bit smaller to allow for mortar joints. But there's an exception to every rule. On this path, the builder wanted a mortared edge, so he bought modular-size bricks. Set in a basket-weave pattern in the middle of the path, they resulted in a more textured look, but many pieces needed to be trimmed.

Choosing a Pattern

Bricks and other rectangular pavers can be arranged in numerous patterns. Jack-on-jack, half-basket-weave, and basket-weave designs eliminate the need to cut pieces, if you lay out the project with square corners and adjust the final edging after the pavers are in place. Herringbone designs require numerous angle cuts, but they are easy to make with a wet saw (see page 29). If you love this look, the added cost of renting the tool may seem insignificant considering all that work you put into excavating and laying a bed of gravel and sand. Herringbone patterns resist movement best and are recommended where cars will drive over the paving.

To make the patterns shown here, the basic pavers need to be half as wide as they are long. Masonry supply companies have patterns that work with pavers of other proportions.

Jack-on-jack	90-degree herringbone	Running bond	Pinwheel
45-degree herringbone	Half-basket weave	Basket weave	Basket weave with 2 × 4 grid

Concrete Paver Ensembles

Many companies sell pavers in mixed pallets, which contain pieces in as many as six different sizes and shapes. These make complicated-looking patterns, but in reality the pieces can be assembled randomly. Sort the pavers first so that you can distribute the various sizes more or less equally. Many concrete pavers come in pallets that include pavers of several different colors, for an overall variegated appearance. You may need to shuffle the pavers so you don't end up with a preponderance of one color in any area.

When paving changes direction, the paver pattern looks best if it accommodates the shift in a way that makes visual sense. In this yard, a running bond pattern makes a seamless transition.

ABOVE: For large rectangular stone pavers, a simple jack-on-jack design works best. Given the variety of colors, a more complicated pattern might have created a look that's too busy.

LEFT: Securely staked invisible edging helps hold these concrete pavers in place. The edging still shows because the path is new, but once the lawn grows a bit, the edge on the right will disappear. A little mulch would cover the edging on the left.

Setting Pavers

The following steps show the procedures to follow if you are installing pavers against solid edging, but you can easily adapt them for situations with invisible edging or edging that you are installing after pavers are set.

Once the bedding is in place (see pages 58–59), do not walk on the sand or disturb it.

1 **START LAYING PAVERS.** Beginning in one corner, set pavers so they abut the edging or adjoining bricks as called for in your pattern. A 90-degree herringbone is shown here. Check the first few pieces to make sure the pavers are ⅛ to ¼ inch higher than you want (they will settle when you tamp them). If they are too low, adjust the screed and screed again. Set each paver straight down. Do not slide them or attempt to adjust their height.

2 **PROGRESS ACROSS THE PAVING.** As you continue to place pavers, periodically measure from a taut mason's line to make sure the paving stays in straight lines. Work on plywood to distribute your weight evenly. Leave gaps where you need to cut pieces to fill along an edge.

3 **REMOVE ANY TEMPORARY GUIDE.** If you installed a temporary screed guide, remove it once you have finished with one section. Spread sand in the next section. Rest one end of the screed on the patio surface and the other end on the edging. Screed the sand and continue laying pavers.

4 **MINIMIZE CUTTING.** You may be able to avoid cutting pavers at one edge by adjusting the edging. Install the pavers up to the end of the patio, then move the edging to abut them. With the pattern shown, some pavers still need to be cut, but only half as many. Trim pavers with one of the methods shown on pages 28–30.

5 **POWER TAMP.** When all of the pavers are in place, run a vibrating plate compactor over the surface to seat the pieces in the bedding sand and force some of the sand up into the bottom of the gaps between pieces. Go over the surface at least two times.

6 **ADD SAND.** Scatter sand over the pavers and use a soft-bristled broom to sweep it into the joints. If the sand is wet, allow it to dry on the surface, then sweep again. Tamp the surface with the plate compactor. Repeat these steps until no more sand disappears into the joints.

Choosing the Right Sand

Bedding sand must be coarse, with a maximum particle size of $3/16$ inch, while joint sand works best if it's fine. If you want to buy only one type, make it bedding sand and count on sweeping off particles too large to fit into joints. Bedding sand is often sold as concrete sand or underlayment sand. Don't use stone dust or mason's sand for mortar, as they don't compact properly with the installation method shown here. For joint sand, you have two choices: plain fine, washed sand and polymer-modified fine sand. The polymer type hardens once it settles into joints and is misted with water. It resists weed growth better than regular sand and doesn't wash out as easily. If your winters are cold, it's better than mixing joint sand with cement, which some people do to make sand joints stronger. The polymers flex if they freeze, while joints with cement crack.

TOP: When you mark the exact center of the edging on two parallel sides of the patio, double-check that the two marks are equidistant from the corners. BOTTOM: Install the first pieces with painstaking precision. If they are slightly out of alignment, the problem will magnify itself over the length of the patio.

Forty-five-Degree Herringbone Pattern

This charming pattern requires careful layout, especially for the first few bricks. Just before you screed the sand for the last time, measure and mark the exact center of the edging on two parallel sides of the patio. Tack a small nail at one of the marks (usually where the patio abuts the house) and hook the clip of a chalk line to the nail. Unroll the chalk line and set it aside. Finish screeding, then pull the chalk line taut between the two marks and snap a line in the sand.

Install the first pavers so their corners just touch the chalk line, as shown. Use an angle square to check that the pavers are 45 degrees to the line. Carefully install a V-shaped row of pavers along the line for about 6 feet. After that, it will be impossible to change the alignment, so ignore the line and just install pavers tight against each other.

If the edging and paver installation is very accurate, you will end up with a large number of cuts that are exactly 45 degrees. However, it is likely that things will move slightly out of alignment, so get an adjustable saw guide when you rent the saw. This will enable you to tinker with the cutting angles.

Other Patterns

Most other patterns, such as basket weave, half-basket weave, and pinwheel, are relatively easy to install, as long as you pay close attention. Every 15 minutes or so, stand back and examine the installation to make sure you didn't make any mistakes.

If you choose a pinwheel pattern, the half-pavers can be of a different material, as long as they are the right size. They must be the same thickness and must not be larger than the width of the other pavers. It's all right if they are slightly smaller.

Grid Patterns

To lay pavers in a framed grid, select a pattern in which full-size pavers completely fill each grid, so that no paver cutting is required. Make sure each framed section of the grid is perfectly square or rectangular.

Estimate the overall size of the patio and excavate the area a little larger than needed. Install wood or timber edging on two adjacent sides. Leave edging pieces a little longer than needed; you will cut them to length later. Add gravel and tamp it well. Build the grid framing using 2 × 4s made of pressure-treated wood or a plastic-wood composite. First install a series of 2 × 4s that run the entire length of the patio, then install short boards between them. Fasten the boards by drilling pilot holes and angle-driving $2\frac{1}{2}$-inch deck screws. Finish the framing by cutting the two edging pieces to fit and filling in with the two remaining pieces.

When you finish the grid, pour and screed sand in each section. Lay the pavers in the pattern of your choice. You may need to trim some pieces to different lengths, perhaps at a slight angle, but the widths should be fine.

TOP: **When you measure for the grid, add $\frac{1}{4}$-inch-thick plywood spacers to create a little extra wiggle room so you're sure that pavers will fit.** BOTTOM: **Use a short screed guide to level the sand at the correct height in each section.**

Curved Path

To lay out a curved path, space the edging so that you can install full-size pavers. This saves time and looks better. Set out a row of pavers as wide as your path. Cut a couple of 2 × 4 spacers to that width, plus $\frac{1}{2}$ inch to accommodate minor discrepancies in the size of the pavers. Use the spacers to align edging while you fasten it with spikes. (Although the edging is being installed on soil in this project, in most instances it should be fastened to a compacted gravel base.)

Position spacers about 3 feet apart as you drive stakes to attach the edging.

MORTARED BRICKS OR PAVERS

MORTARED PAVING NEEDS TO HAVE CONCRETE UNDERNEATH. The concrete can be new or old, but if it's old, it must be stable. Minor cracks are okay, but if sections have settled unevenly, don't waste your time and money trying to make it look better by adding pavers on top. The cracks will eventually transfer into the mortared layer. Instead, replace the slab or consult a company that specializes in injecting concrete under slabs to raise them to equal height. Of course, you can also opt to remove the damaged concrete and pour a fresh slab.

When you set paving in mortar, thin pieces work fine. For paver pattern ideas, see page 60. Plan your design so that the top layer reflects any control joints in the underlying concrete.

Mortar mixes named for every other letter in the term "mason work" vary in strength and workability. The three most common types are M, S, and N. O and K are also mortar types, but they are for specialized work. Of the kinds suitable for the projects in this book, M is the highest strength, S is next, and N is of moderate strength, which makes it the best choice for most garden walls. For outdoor paving, S is best, though M and N also work.

For the following method, install permanent edging or temporary 2 × 4 forms so you have a screed guide. The edging or forms should be higher than the slab by the thickness of a paver plus $1/2$ inch. Dampen the bricks several hours beforehand.

1 **SCREED MORTAR OVER THE CONCRETE.** Make a screed out of a 2 × 4 and a piece of plywood (see page 58). The plywood should extend downward $1/4$ inch less than the thickness of a paver.

If the concrete is old, clean it thoroughly. Take special care to remove any oil residue. Allow the surface to dry, then coat it with concrete bonding adhesive, which resembles white glue and may be labeled as a concrete fortifier. Follow the manufacturer's instructions. Usually you need to wait for the bonding agent to dry at least partially. If the concrete is new, dampen it.

Prepare bagged mortar mix in a wheelbarrow or a mixing trough, or in a large plastic bucket if you have a paddle mixer and a drill. The mortar should cling to a trowel. Working in an area about 5 feet square, shovel the mortar onto the slab and smooth it with the screed guide.

2 **SET THE PAVERS.** Using scraps of ³/₈-inch plywood as spacers, set the pavers in the mortar. They will settle slightly as you install them. Lay a flat board on top and tap with a hammer to bed the pavers and produce a flat surface.

3 **FILL THE JOINTS USING A MORTAR BAG.** The next day, fill a grout bag with the same type of mortar you used the day before. Squeeze the bag to squirt mortar into the joints. Keep folding the bag over as you work.

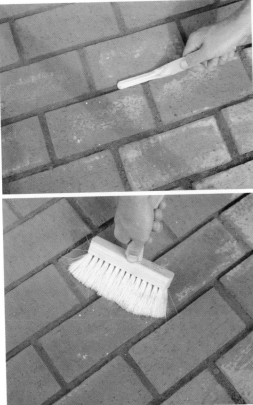

4 **TOOL THE JOINTS.** Once you have completed a 5-foot-square section, use a jointer to compress the mortar and smooth the joints. Tool the long joints first, then the short ones.

5 **CLEAN THE JOINTS.** When the mortar is fairly dry, brush it lightly with a mason's brush. Take care not to brush any wet mortar, or you will smear it. Fill in any voids and holes with mortar, using the jointer to work in the mortar. After several hours, clean the surface using a mason's brush and water. After a week or so, apply sealer to the entire surface.

Installing Pavers on Concrete Without Mortar

Instead of setting bricks or other pavers in mortar on a concrete base, you can install them in a way that mimics the look of pavers set on a gravel base with sand joints. At the perimeter of the concrete, install permanent edging approximately equal to the height of the pavers. Spread two layers of No. 30 building felt (tar paper) to cushion the bricks and compensate for minor surface irregularities. Place the bricks, then sweep sand into the joints. Mist to settle the sand and then add more sand until the paving is stiff. You can also use this method to cover asphalt paving with pavers.

FLAGSTONES ON CONCRETE

MORTARING FLAGSTONES TO CONCRETE is slightly more complicated than topping concrete with brick or other pavers. Because flagstones come in irregular shapes, they require more fitting and cutting. You also need to adjust the mortar to account for their uneven thickness.

See page 10 for tips on buying flagstone. Sort the stones into several piles according to size. When you lay out the stones, choose some from each pile so that you end up with an even distribution of large, medium, and small pieces. Pick out the thickest pieces and use them to determine the finished height of the paving.

You can install edging for this kind of a project, but natural edges look great and require less cutting. If you want an irregular edge, allow stones to overhang the concrete a few inches where necessary.

1 **PREPARE THE CONCRETE.** Clean the concrete thoroughly, especially any oil spills, and allow it to dry. Brush on concrete bonding adhesive and wait as the label instructs.

2 **LAY STONES IN A DRY RUN.** Using at least one of the thickest pieces, fill in a 9-square-foot area with dry-laid stones. Aim for joints that are roughly uniform, about $1/2$ to 1 inch wide. Don't let adjacent stones touch. You may need to shuffle and reorient the stones to get the right fit. If a stone needs to be cut, mark it and make the cut with one of the methods shown on pages 29–30.

3 **PREPARE THE MORTAR AND SET STONES.** Prepare a batch of mortar mix that's thick enough to cling for a second or two to a shovel held vertically. Move a thick stone to the side and spread about $1/2$ inch of mortar where it was. Press the stone down lightly into the mortar. Repeat with more stones. Make sure each new stone is approximately level and at the same height as its neighbors.

4 **CHECK AND ADJUST THE ALIGNMENT.** As you complete the section, use a long, straight board to make sure stones are even. Place a level on the board to check for the proper slope. Make any needed adjustments immediately, before the mortar starts to set. If a stone doesn't move easily, or if it is too low, remove it, apply more mortar, and reset it. If the mortar stiffens before you use it all, throw it out and make a new batch.

5 **FILL THE JOINTS.** Carefully use a mason's trowel or a grout bag (see page 67) to slip mortar into the joints. Gently scrape with a small piece of wood to provide an even fill. After the mortar has started to dry, lightly brush away crumbs. Wait a few more hours, then scrub the stones with water, a stiff bristle brush, and a rag. Or, if you live where winters are mild and you want a more natural look, sweep in fine, crushed stone, as shown. Set a garden hose nozzle to "mist" and spray the entire surface. Allow the surface to dry, then sweep in more crushed stone to fill any gaps, and mist again.

Shortcut System

Although the standard advice calls for a full concrete slab under mortared paving, if you live where the climate is mild, you can pour the concrete little by little instead as you install paving. Lay a gravel base and compact it well with a vibrating plate compactor. Trial-fit pieces and cut them as necessary, then prepare a bag of sand mix or mortar mix. (Don't use standard concrete mix with gravel.) Move the stones out of the way, add the concrete mixture, and replace the stones. Adjust them until they are the right height and are properly sloped. Let them sit undisturbed until the mortar hardens, then fill the joints with mortar.

Pebble mosaic artist Jeffrey Bale of Portland, Oregon, sets mortared paving on a bed of mortar, with only a compacted gravel base underneath. After working on projects throughout the West for years, he says he's had no complaints about cracking or stones slipping askew.

TILING OVER CONCRETE

HANDMADE CLAY TILES OR STONE TILES WITH NATURALLY SPLIT SURFACES look great in a garden setting. But accommodating the size variation requires a slightly different installation process than you'd use for the factory-made tiles that are more common indoors. This project features handmade saltillo tiles, which are popular where winters are warm. They are too porous to survive a freezing winter. The procedure also applies to stone tile with slightly irregular dimensions. These saltillos were glazed at the factory. If you are using unglazed saltillos or porous stone, apply a sealer before you install them to prevent mortar stains.

Sort the tiles before you begin. Set aside warped pieces with a slight hump in the center until you have mortar prepared and can spread a little, like frosting, to make the backs flat. If thickness varies significantly, sort out the thicker pieces and include at least one in each section you set so that the paving turns out even.

Before tiling a concrete slab, be sure it is stable. Deep cracks are likely to show up in your tiled surface, even if you patch first. Run a straightedge along the surface and knock down any protrusions with a hammer and chisel or a grinder. Patch large holes, clean the concrete, let it dry, then paint the surface with concrete bonding adhesive.

1 **LAY OUT THE PROJECT.** Check the slab to make sure corners are square (see pages 38–39). If not, draw two lines at a 90-degree angle to each other and make all your measurements from them. Do a test run by placing tiles to make a section about 3 feet square. Space them to allow grout lines of a width you want. Measure the width of the tiles plus one extra grout line. This is the size of the squares in which the tiles should be laid. Using a tape measure and chalk line, mark lines in both directions to produce a grid of squares.

2 **TROWEL ON THE MORTAR.** Mix a batch of latex-reinforced mortar so it is just stiff enough to cling for a second or two to a trowel held vertically. Using a notched trowel of the size recommended by the tile dealer, spread the mortar inside one of the squares. First spread a thick layer using the flat side of the trowel. Then use the notched side to comb the mortar. Don't scrape down to the concrete.

3 **PLACE AND ALIGN THE TILES.** Fill the square with tiles, leaving gaps for grout lines. Set the tiles straight down into the mortar; don't slide them or press down on them. Stand up and examine the tiles from several angles to be sure the grout lines are as consistent and straight as possible.

4 **BED THE TILES AND CHECK ADHESION.** Place a block of wood or a piece of plywood across several tiles and gently tap it to seat the pieces evenly. Every so often, pick up a tile to make sure the mortar is sticking to at least three-quarters of the back surface. If it's not, back-butter each tile with a thin layer of mortar before setting it in the troweled mortar.

5 **CUT TILES TO FIT.** At edges, you may need to trim some pieces. Cut tiles using a rented wet saw, or a grinder or circular saw equipped with a masonry cutting blade or a diamond blade. Some tiles are easier to cut with a snap cutter. Ask your tile dealer which cutting tool to use.

6 **GROUT AND CLEAN.** Wait about 2 days for the mortar to harden. Mix a batch of latex-reinforced sanded grout just to the point that it does not pour readily. If joints are 3/8 inch or wider, apply the grout with a mortar bag and shape the joints with a brick tool or the rounded end of a trowel handle (see page 67). If joints are narrow, hold a laminated grout float nearly flat and push grout between the tiles in at least two directions. When the joints in an area are full, tilt the float up and use it to squeegee away most of the excess grout. Drag a wet towel over the area, then wipe lightly with a damp sponge, rinsed often. Once the grout starts to stiffen, use the sponge to shape the surface to a consistent depth. Allow the surface to dry until a white haze appears, then buff it away with a dry cloth. Mist the grout with water until damp and cover it with plastic for several days, making sure it stays damp.

PEBBLE MOSAICS

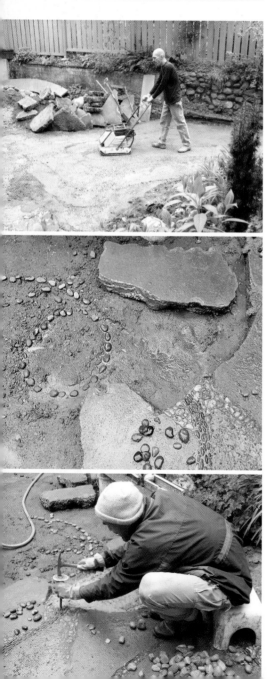

BY USING PEBBLES AS MOSAIC MATERIAL, you can create paving with the richly detailed look of a tapestry. The designs may look delicate, but they're actually very durable. Jeffrey Bale of Portland, Oregon, who has built pebble mosaics throughout the West, developed the method shown here.

Building a pebble mosaic takes more time and more material than you might expect. Start with a small project. Also consider buying the pebbles by the bag or in bulk rather than trying to collect them a couple of pocketfuls at a time. Sort for color and size before you embark on construction. Dampen pebbles before you set them.

A pebble mosaic must be constructed on a firm base. An existing concrete slab makes an excellent substrate. A compacted gravel bed also works, especially where soil does not freeze. When you get to the mortaring-in stage, work in the shade or on a cool day, or set up an umbrella so you aren't working in the hot sun.

1 **PREPARE THE BASE.** Prepare the base, then add and compact the gravel, as shown on pages 42–43. Bale uses gravel $\frac{1}{4}$ inch in diameter and smaller. After alternately misting it with water and tamping it with a vibrating plate compactor, he spreads about an inch of sand so he can trace the design in it.

2 **ESTABLISH THE DESIGN.** Trace the main features of the design in the sand, then temporarily place pebbles along the lines so you can stand back and make sure you are satisfied. This project is an extension of a patio with a design that evokes paintings by Joan Miro, a Spanish surrealist. Swirling black lines weave around large chunks of recycled concrete.

3 **ENSURE A CLEAN BREAK.** Most pebble mosaics can't be done in a day. Where old mortar slopes off along an edge, Bale chips it off so the new mortar will go against a vertical surface. Otherwise, there might not be enough room for the new pebbles to seat properly, or they might not fit tightly against the existing mosaic. Bale avoids back strain by working on a low stool.

4 MIX AND ADD MORTAR. Prepare a sack of Type S mortar mix using one of the methods shown on pages 90–91. Add just enough water so that the mortar holds together but does not slump when you set down a handful. Bale pats the mortar against the adjoining concrete or other edging, but leaves a gap at the top for pebbles.

5 SET PEBBLES. Starting next to an edge or area previously set, place pebbles that establish the design. Set each piece into the mortar with a thin edge facing up, then tightly butt the pieces to each other or to an edge. Push each stone into the mortar so that at least two-thirds of the stone is embedded. As you work, you may have to add mortar or shove mortar to the side to maintain a fairly consistent height.

6 ADD FILL STONES. Once the main design pieces are in place, fill in background areas. The background stones in this design are rounded and light-colored, so they contrast well with the thin, black outline stones. Set them vertically, with a thin edge up.

7 LEVEL THE STONES. Stop placing stones when you are a few inches back from the outside edge of the mortar. (The excess serves as a temporary dam, which you'll remove as you move on to the next area.) Place plywood over the area and press down to seat all stones to the same level as nearby paving. Bale applies pressure by stepping on the board.

8 RINSE OFF EXCESS MORTAR. Using a soft spray from a hose, rinse excess mortar from the surface. Use as little water as possible. When the mortar stiffens, cut back the excess with a trowel and repeat steps 3 through 8. Cover the mosaic with plastic and keep the surface moist so that the mortar cures slowly. The next day, scrub off any mortar that sticks to the face of the stones. If a whitish haze remains, wait a month, then clean with a muriatic acid solution.

PERVIOUS PAVING

PERVIOUS PAVING, ALSO KNOWN AS POROUS OR PERMEABLE PAVING, lets rainwater drain into a deep gravel layer underneath. It's a "green" option because the water slowly percolates through the paving into the soil, reducing stormwater runoff that carries pollutants into local water supplies and replenishing groundwater. There's also the benefit of having no puddles on top of your path or patio during the rainy season.

Installing pervious paving is similar to working with other pavers, except that the base and bedding layers differ. The base gravel is deep, often 2 feet or more, and consists of round particles with diameters that range between those of nickels and quarters. In the gravel industry, the ideal is known as No. 57 rock. The bedding layer, immediately under the pavers, consists of finer gravel, about ⅜ inch in diameter. The same material fills gaps between pavers. Pervious paving systems don't include sand.

Pervious paving can be used to cover large areas and can handle considerable runoff, including gutter water. But releasing too much water next to a building could create a problem in a basement or crawl space. The project shown here, a landing for steps to a basement, handles only the water that falls there as rain. Though enough to create a puddle on the old concrete landing, it isn't enough to seep into the basement.

Pervious paving normally requires edging (see pages 46–53), but this project already had concrete on all sides.

1 **EXCAVATE TO DEPTH.** Pervious paving requires a relatively deep excavation so that water can pool during storms. For a large project, especially one involving roof runoff, a soils engineer should calculate the required depth. For this small project, 2 feet is deep enough.

2 **ADD FILTER FABRIC.** Line the bottom and sides of the excavation with filter fabric to keep fine clay particles from flowing into the gravel and plugging the spaces between stones. Drape excess fabric over the edges and anchor it with rocks, or pin the fabric to walls of the excavation with rebar ties clipped in half.

3 **ADD DRAIN ROCK.** Fill most of the excavation with drainage rock, ideally round, washed particles that are approximately 1 inch in diameter. An improvised plywood chute speeds the work. After you add each 4 inches of gravel, rake it level and tamp it with a vibrating plate compactor or a hand tamper. The final height should allow room for about 1½ inches of finer gravel plus the pavers.

4 **ADD BEDDING GRAVEL.** Add the ³⁄₈-inch gravel and rake it level. Do not tamp it.

5 **SET THE PAVERS.** Place the first row of pavers and determine where any necessary cuts will be made. If pavers are wider on one end than on the other, turn each end piece before penciling a line to show the excess.

6 **CUT THE PAVERS.** Hand-cutting methods don't work well on concrete pavers. Make cuts with a rented wet saw. Use the sliding table to support the block.

7 **TAMP.** To seat the pavers evenly, tamp the surface with a vibrating plate compactor or hand tamper.

8 **FILL GAPS.** Sprinkle more bedding gravel onto the paving and sweep it into gaps between the pavers.

CREATING STEPS

STEPS ON A PATH OR NEXT TO A PATIO serve a multitude of purposes. Besides easing people up and down slopes, they add a bit of drama and help define separate areas of a garden. If you have a gentle slope, or if you need only a couple of steps in a rustic setting, a few large stone slabs might be the perfect solution. But other situations call for building more complete staircases, with handrails and perhaps even lighting on treads. Lighting is particularly useful when there are just a few steps along a path, because people aren't expecting them.

In designing steps, you have a series of decisions to make. Possible materials range from timber to concrete, brick, or stone. You'll need a strategy to prevent dirt from washing down the slope onto your steps. For example, you could bury stones halfway at both sides of the steps, or you could build a low retaining wall alongside them. And, in most cases, you'll want to select plants to add next to the stairs.

A grand entry staircase picks up the same colors as the stone used to create terraces on a 6-foot-high slope at this Santa Fe house.

From the top, you can see how the stones are mortared together and how they show off the surrounding landscape.

ABOVE: Textural contrasts are one of the delights of this staircase, which rises from smooth bluestone paving alongside a retaining wall built of closely fitted ashlar blocks.

BELOW: Stackable retaining blocks, originally designed for building mortarless retaining walls, can also be used to make garden steps.

ABOVE: For a unified look, brick is a good choice, as it can be used to create walls, paving, and steps.

Designing a Stairway

The reason some steps are pleasant to climb while others feel awkward probably stems from their proportions. A handy formula sums up what works: At each step, the run (or distance you move forward) plus twice the rise (the elevation you gain) should equal 25 to 27 inches. So if each step rises a short distance, the part you walk on should be relatively deep. If each step is tall, the tread will be shallower.

For outdoor steps, the rise can range from 4 to 7 inches. Stair treads should be at least 13 inches deep. The ideal combination, according to some landscape architects, is 6-inch risers with 15-inch treads.

To keep people from tripping, the rise and run must be consistent for all steps in a staircase, although there's a little leeway on rustic steps. Keeping the height uniform is the most important thing. Uniform tread depth also matters, but it's not as critical. To break a fall if someone trips, and to give people a place to catch their breath, divide long flights into sections with no more than five steps between landings whenever possible.

Stone tiles pave a staircase that's easy to use because treads are deep and uniformly spaced. The more refined the staircase, the more important it becomes for all steps to be precisely the same height. People will expect to use the steps as they would an indoor staircase, so any irregularity could cause someone to trip.

To lay out stairs, first determine the total rise and run. On short slopes, extend a level board across the slope and mark the beginning and end of the steps. The distance between these marks is the total run. Measure down from the end mark to determine the total rise. If the slope is too long to span with a board, divide the slope into shorter sections and add up individual measurements, or use a line level and stakes to set a level length of mason's twine as your reference point. If you plan to provide a landing stone or paving at the top of the slope, or a foundation stone that's slightly out of the ground at the bottom, be sure to adjust your measurements to take that into account.

Next, decide what riser height you'd like, keeping it between 4 and 7 inches. Divide that into the total rise (in inches). Round off the fraction and you'll have the number of steps you need.

Divide the number of steps into the total rise. The answer is the exact riser height you need.

Divide the total run by the number of steps to get the run of each step. In some cases, this also equals the depth of treads. But you'll need deeper treads if you want an overhang on the front and space at the back to support the next riser.

Massive stone slabs, each the thickness of one tread, lead up to a sitting area. Because these steps aren't used frequently, they also harbor hearty plants. Outdoor steps with a rugged texture like this signal to people that they should slow down and watch where they step. People are more likely to trip on steps that appear to be regular but really aren't.

If you can't get the calculations to result in steps with the proper dimensions, you might need to "stretch" the slope by building the steps at an angle across the slope or by creating a zigzag route with several landings. Or you might need to shorten the slope by building up soil at the bottom or cutting away soil at the top.

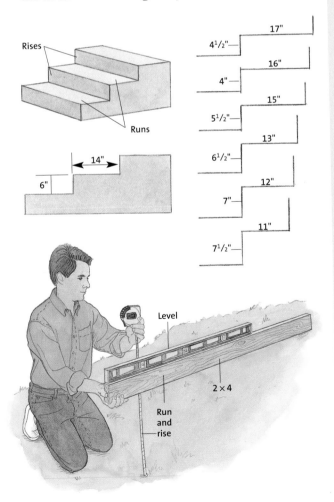

Simple Steps

Massive stones approximately equal in thickness make attractive steps. Where there is good access for heavy equipment, use relatively flat pieces that are 4 to 7 inches thick and deep enough so the back 3 inches of each step can support the front of the step above. Buy an extra piece for a foundation.

At the bottom of the slope, dig a foundation hole as big around as the stone. Make it as deep as the stone if your winters are mild or, if your soil freezes, 4 to 6 inches deeper so you can pack in gravel. Over the soil or gravel, pack damp sand into a 2-inch layer. Move in the foundation stone and adjust it so it doesn't wobble. The top should be 2 inches above the ground and sloped slightly downhill.

Excavate, add a sand layer, and set each succeeding step in rising order. Rest the front of each stone on the back of the one below. If stones wobble, add or remove sand, or shim under the front edge with small, flat stones.

Before and after pictures of the same staircase show the wisdom of digging back some of the bank alongside the steps. Adding plants or large stones there helps keep soil from washing onto the steps.

FLAGSTONE OR PAVER STEPS

THESE STEPS CAN TAKE ON DIFFERENT LOOKS, depending on the materials you use. Treads can be flagstones, bluestone pavers, or concrete pavers $1\frac{1}{2}$ to 2 inches thick, and they can be large slabs or pieces that you mortar together. For risers, options include granite cobblestones, ledgestone, or several layers of brick or stone mortared together. Determine the height of the riser material by subtracting the thickness of the treads from the per-step rise that you will calculate in step 1 below. You also need rectangular stones to hold back soil at the sides of each step, plus gravel, concrete, and mortar.

If you need to mortar pieces together to create the treads, create tread-size arrangements before you begin building, so you don't have to stop to cut pieces. Leave about $\frac{1}{2}$ inch between pieces for mortar. Each tread should be big enough to allow a 1-inch overhang in the front and a space of perhaps 3 inches in the back to support the riser of the next step.

1 **LAY OUT THE STEPS.** Extend a level string or board across the slope and calculate the total rise and run of the steps, as described on pages 78–79. Mark off increments on the string or board to show the run, or depth, of each step.

Transfer these marks to the ground with a plumb bob on a string. Drive a stake into each spot. Use a carpenter's square to lay out parallel lines and establish the other side of the steps. Drive stakes at those corners too.

2 **EXCAVATE.** With a shovel, remove enough soil to create the rough shape of the steps.

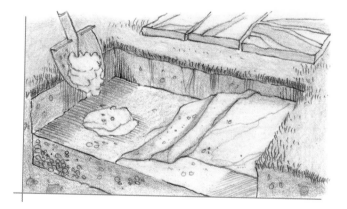

3 **CREATE THE FOUNDATION.** Arrange the flagstones that will cover the foundation, which will be flush with the soil. Mark the overall outline, remove the stones, and dig down 11 inches. Pack the hole with 4 inches of gravel.

Prepare bagged concrete mix and shovel it over the gravel, making a 4-inch layer walled in by soil. Smooth the surface (it doesn't need to be perfect) and wait at least 24 hours.

4 **SET ANGLED STONES AND ADD FLAGSTONE TO THE BASE.** Near the back of the foundation, dig out on each side so you can place one rectangular cobblestone at a 45-degree angle to keep dirt from falling in on the sides. Set the stones far enough forward so they won't be completely covered by the risers of the next step.

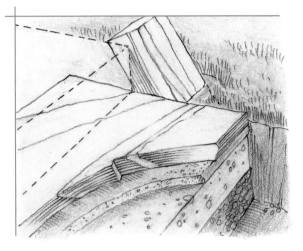

Prepare bagged mortar mix or a homemade batch of 1 part masonry cement to 3 parts masonry sand. Add just enough water to create a stiff mix. Spread a 2-inch layer on the concrete and around the angled stone. Top this with the flagstones. Tap them with a rubber mallet until they are even and sloped slightly toward the front.

With a trowel, fill spaces between stones with mortar. When it stiffens slightly, cut off any excess mortar with the towel and lift the material away. Clean up residue with a damp sponge. Cover the project with plastic and wait three days.

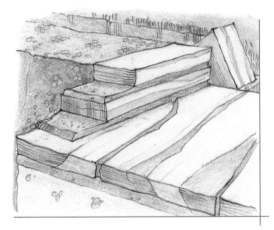

5 **ADD RISER STONES.** To build the next step, spread a 1-inch layer of mortar along the back of the finished tread. Install the riser stones and fill between them with mortar. Level the stones and wipe away any spilled mortar.

6 **FINISH THE STEPS.** After the mortar sets, carefully dig a 6-inch-deep hole behind the riser to accommodate the next step. Add 3 inches of gravel, tamp it, then add more gravel and tamp again. Stop when the gravel is 2 inches below the top of the riser. Mix mortar and spread a 2-inch layer over the crushed gravel. Set the flagstones for the next tread in place, with 1 inch overhanging the riser below. Tap the stones to seat them, making sure they are level. Fill in the joints with mortar and finish them as shown on page 67. Repeat the process for the remaining steps.

concrete

RELATIVELY INEXPENSIVE BUT DURABLE, POURED CONCRETE IS ONE
OF THE MOST POPULAR OPTIONS FOR GARDEN PAVING. POURING
THE CONCRETE YOURSELF IS NOT A JOB TO BE TAKEN LIGHTLY, AS
A MISTAKE IN PLANNING OR EXECUTION CAN LEAD TO A PROBLEM
THAT IS DIFFICULT TO CORRECT. HOWEVER, IT'S ALSO NOT AS
DAUNTING AS MANY PEOPLE ASSUME. THIS CHAPTER SHOWS
WHAT'S INVOLVED SO YOU CAN DECIDE WHETHER TO TAKE ON A
JOB AND, IF SO, HOW TO DO IT RIGHT.

DESIGN OPTIONS

CONCRETE IS AMAZINGLY VERSATILE when you use it to build paths and patios. Provided you build a suitable form, it will harden into any shape you want. You can change its standard gray color by adding pigment along with the other ingredients, or by staining the surface once the slab is poured. You can also dress up its look by exposing gravel or sand that's within the mix, or by sprinkling decorative pebbles on the surface while the concrete is still pliable. And a wide array of specialty tools allow you to press textured designs into the surface.

Some options include practical considerations, as well as aesthetic issues. If you live where the soil freezes often, for example, highly textured concrete might not be as durable as smooth concrete. Textured areas trap water, which expands as it turns to ice, and that in turn can cause the surface to disintegrate.

However, on a patio next to a pool, texture improves traction. It also makes the concrete seem cooler when barefoot kids run over it, because less surface area is in contact with their feet. Exposing pebbles on the surface also improves traction, and it makes concrete more resistant to wear and stains because the characteristics of the pebbles become the dominant factor.

Individually poured slabs separated by planting strips can form a patio. Just keep the paving in a size that works with the footprint of the furniture.

BELOW: This exposed-aggregate path was divided into manageable sections, each of which could be poured separately. After the forms were removed, the intervening spaces were filled with plants. A path like this is a good solution for a gentle slope where you don't want actual steps, because each pad can be a slightly different elevation.

RIGHT: This is a poured-concrete path, but it looks like rustic stone, thanks to the rough texture and the irregular shapes of the pieces. The path was poured as a slab, then cut. Spaces were filled with soil and planted with moss.

Appearing to hover a few inches off the ground, this concrete patio makes the surrounding gravel look like a dry creek bed. To pour a slab like this, make most of it thick, but form the edges so that the bottom is indented 6 inches or so.

BELOW: A rock-salt finish adds traction and a design element to this poolside patio. The texture is created with rock salt that's pressed into newly poured concrete immediately after it is floated smooth. After 24 hours, the salt is rinsed and brushed away.

RIGHT: Unadorned except for the smooth pattern created by an edging tool, this path curves gracefully toward the front door. The newly poured concrete was lightly scored with broom bristles before the edging tool was used for the last time, creating the subtle difference in textures.

CONCRETE BASICS

MANY PEOPLE USE THE TERMS "CEMENT" AND "CONCRETE" INTERCHANGEABLY, but the two materials are not the same. Cement is just glue. Concrete is what you get by mixing cement with aggregate (usually gravel and sand) and enough water to produce a workable consistency. A basic recipe calls for 1 part cement, 2 parts pea gravel, 2 parts sand, and $\frac{1}{2}$ part water. Some mixes also incorporate fibers, acrylic fortifiers, and other additives.

The most common cement, known as portland cement, is usually gray. White cement is also available, though at a higher price. Pigments mixed with gray cement result in muted colors, while those mixed with white cement make brighter colors.

Gravel and sand, known collectively as aggregate, fill most of the space in concrete and give it most of its strength. A range of particle sizes works best because small pieces fit between big ones. However, the biggest particles should not exceed one-fifth the thickness of the concrete, or it may break apart. If you are mixing concrete for paths and patios $3\frac{1}{2}$ to 4 inches thick, that means you should use nothing larger than $\frac{3}{4}$ inch in diameter. For the sand, use mason's sand or all-purpose sand, both of which contain sharp-edged particles in various sizes. Avoid play sand, which has round grains of fairly uniform size.

In most poured-concrete projects, you don't really see the sand and gravel. They're submerged under a surface skim of fine sand and cement, plus any pigment. However, if you are planning to expose the aggregate or sprinkle decorative pebbles on the surface, you might want to purchase aggregate in specific colors.

Professionals check consistency by filling a testing cone with concrete and measuring how much the concrete slumps when the cone is removed. For a simple version of this test, cut the bottom off a plastic cup and set the cup upside down. Fill it with concrete and remove the cup by lifting straight up. If the concrete slumps to about three-fourths of its former height in the cup, the mix is right for pouring into a form.

The amount of water plays a big role in determining how strong the concrete turns out. Adding too much makes concrete easier to shape, but it weakens the mixture because the excess water creates tiny, permanent tunnels as it goes to the surface to evaporate. Excess water also increases the risk of tiny cracks appearing on the surface.

To avoid these problems yet still have concrete that flows well, replace some of the water in the recipe with acrylic or latex fortifier, or use concrete bonding adhesive, which is basically the same thing. Do not use these products with bagged mixes that specify adding only water, however. If you order concrete delivered in a mixer truck, you can ask to have a water-reducing additive included. The mixing company can also add pozzolans, which are specialty cements such as fly ash and metakaolin. They act like miniature BBs and help other ingredients slip into place with less water.

Once cement stiffens, abundant moisture is good. It allows hydration, the chemical reaction that hardens concrete, to continue. Once the concrete dries, however, hydration ceases. Adding more water at that point won't restart the reaction.

Properly mixed concrete is completely wet but isn't soupy. If you pick some up (wearing gloves) and squeeze it, it should roughly hold its shape, and liquid should not drip from your fingers.

Decoding Bagged Mixes

Labels on bagged concrete mixes can help point you to the right product for a specific job. The strength (shown as psi, or pounds per square inch) refers specifically to crush resistance, but you can use it as an overall indicator of durability and abrasion resistance. The higher the number, the better.

Sand mix contains no gravel, just portland cement and sand in a 1:3 ratio. Use it for stepping-stones or pavers 1 1/2 to 2 inches thick, or for topping old concrete. Toppings can be as thin as 1/2 inch if you replace half of the usual water with acrylic or latex fortifier.

This basic mix of portland cement, sand, and gravel is suitable for objects at least 2 inches thick. You can use it for wall foundations, steps, or paths. But its lean cement content means it's relatively difficult to trowel to a smooth finish.

Concrete resurfacing mix contains portland cement, fine sand, polymers, and other ingredients. Use it up to 1/2 inch thick as a layer over old concrete. The material is quite fluid, so you can spread it with a trowel, brush, or squeegee.

A high-early-strength concrete mix contains a higher percentage of portland cement, plus sand, gravel, and additives. It's for the same type of projects as basic concrete mix, but the extra cement makes a smooth finish easier to create.

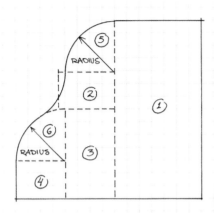

ABOVE: To calculate volumes for complex shapes, divide the space into slabs and parts of cylinders. Note how area 2 is treated as a slab. Areas 5 and 6 are each one-fourth of a cylinder, so calculate their volume (height × 3.14 × radius^2) as if they were cylinders, then divide by 4.

Calculating How Much Concrete You Need

Concrete is sold by volume. To calculate the amount you need, multiply your object's length times its width times its height. Measure the height in several spots to get a reliable average, because a discrepancy of even $1/2$ inch can make a big difference in the amount you need.

If your project has a complex shape, mentally divide it into slabs and parts of cylinders and calculate the volume for each section. For a slab, the formula is length times width times height. Treat curved areas as squat cylinders. Multiply the radius by itself, then by 3.14 (the numerical value known as pi), and finally by the height. Contractor's calculators automatically convert feet and inches to the decimal system. If you're using old-fashioned math or a standard calculator, multiply the length and width in feet by the depth in inches. After you multiply those numbers to get the volume, divide by 12 to get the number of cubic feet. Labels on bagged mixes usually state yield that way. Convert to cubic yards (for truck delivery) by dividing the total volume in cubic feet by 27. Order 10 percent more than you think you'll need.

Preventing Cracks

Some concrete objects need metal or fiber reinforcement to keep them from cracking. Others do fine without it. Understanding why concrete cracks and how reinforcement works will help you decide when to add it. When in doubt, put it in. Reinforcement is cheap insurance.

When this concrete paving's support eroded, it cracked from lack of stiffness.

Cracks caused by lack of stiffness are the most serious. On paths and patios or in foundations for garden walls, they occur mostly when soil underneath settles or erodes. Where there is no soil, the concrete needs to function almost like a bridge. Under a heavy load, it begins to bend or stretch. Concrete can't bend much, so it relieves the stress by cracking. Metal reinforcement, such as rebar, helps prevent this by adding stiffness. Even if it's not enough to keep cracks from forming, the rebar still ties the pieces together so they're less likely to settle unevenly and cause a person to trip or a wall to tilt. Metal reinforcement is usually added to patios and foundations but not to paths, because the narrow span of a path creates less potential for the bridge scenario.

Small surface cracks are caused by excess water in the mix. These cracks don't develop into tripping hazards, but they are unsightly. Prevent them by limiting how much water you use and by adding thin fibers with the other ingredients. Polypropylene fibers (shown at right), the most common kind used in concrete, separate in a mixer into countless fine strands. A 1-pound bag is enough to prevent surface cracks in half a cubic yard or even a full cubic yard of concrete.

Adding too much water to the initial mix resulted in these surface cracks.

Cracks caused by shrinkage stem from the fact that concrete slowly contracts as it loses water while drying. Long, skinny rectangles and interior corners on L-shaped objects are especially prone to cracking. Avoid problems by redesigning your project into squares and short rectangles, or cut grooves in the hardening concrete so that sections have stable shapes. To determine where joints or grooves need to be, multiply the slab's thickness in inches by $2\frac{1}{2}$. The result is the maximum number of feet that should be in a section. For example, a pathway or patio 4 inches thick requires a break every 10 feet. If you saw the joints, make them 1 inch deep in a slab $3\frac{1}{2}$ or 4 inches deep. Cut them with a diamond blade in a circular saw after the concrete cures for a day or two.

To round a corner, this concrete walkway was cast into an L shape. It cracked at the corner.

If you can't avoid weak shapes, reinforce them with rebar or welded-wire mesh to help the concrete move as one piece.

Creating Freeze-Resistant Concrete

Ice crystals occupy about 9 percent more space than the water that's in them. So when concrete absorbs water and then freezes, the ice can literally split the concrete. Each of these steps eliminates or at least reduces this concern:

• ADD AN AIR-ENTRAINING PRODUCT. Available from concrete-supply companies, this material forms tiny bubbles that act as safety valves, giving ice crystals room to expand. Requires truck delivery or motorized mixing.

• REPLACE SOME OF THE MIX WATER with acrylic or latex fortifier.

• BARELY DAMPEN THE CONCRETE when you mix it. Pound the mixture into place.

• USE A BAGGED MIX that contains waterproofing ingredients.

• COAT THE CURED CONCRETE with a sealer.

Mix It Yourself or Have It Delivered?

As with food, you can mix up a batch of concrete from scratch, use a bagged mix (the equivalent of a just-add-water cake mix), or go the order-in route and arrange for delivery of concrete that's ready to put into a mold. The best option depends on the size of your project, access to the site, and other factors.

Truck delivery saves you the effort of mixing the ingredients and cleaning the tools, and it ensures that all the concrete is evenly blended. If your project is within reach of the mixer truck's chute—often about 18 feet—it also saves you from having to move the wet concrete in wheelbarrows.

Standard revolving-barrel mixers usually won't deliver less than 1 cubic yard—enough concrete for a 4-inch-thick patio 8 by 10 feet. In some areas, short-pour trucks are also available. These carry ingredients in separate bins and mix them at the job site, so you can order smaller amounts. Renting a trailer from a company that also supplies the premixed concrete is a third option.

If you want to mix the concrete yourself, weigh the pros and cons of starting from scratch versus using a bagged mix. Mixing from scratch saves money. However, cement comes only in 94-pound sacks, while mixes typically weigh just 40 or 60 pounds a bag. If you have a bad back, this difference might matter more than the cost. Storage is another issue. Bagged mixes need to be kept in a dry area but are fairly compact, while piles of aggregate can be left out in the weather but occupy a lot of space. Bagged mixes also help ensure consistency from batch to batch.

Choosing a Mixing Method

Whether you are preparing concrete from scratch or using a bagged mix, you have a choice of mixing methods.

Hand mixing requires only a hoe or a shovel, plus a wheelbarrow or a mortar tray. Because a wheelbarrow is elevated and a tray rests on the ground, each allows a different working angle. Experiment to discover which you prefer. Pour the dry ingredients into one end and the water into the other, then gradually work the dry material into the moist area.

Standard portable mixers have a revolving drum, which mixes well when gravel is among the ingredients. (Sand mixes tend to become plastered on the sides.) Put in about three-fourths of the water first, along with liquid pigment if you are

For hand mixing, pull the dry mixture into the water little by little with a hoe or a shovel. Work the dampened material back toward the dry area, almost as if you were kneading bread. With the tool blade, repeatedly slice through the mixture to break up any lumps.

using it. Add gravel, then any dry pigment you are using, then sand and finally cement. Mix after each addition. After you add the cement, squirt one burst of water into the mixer to reduce dust and prevent clumps. Tilt the tub back and forth periodically as the machine mixes. Add the final water in small amounts.

Rental companies carry portable mixers that operate on electricity or gasoline. A 3.5-cubic-foot mixer fits in the back of a pickup and handles several bags of concrete mix, but not 3.5 cubic feet. You must leave air space. Larger mixers need to be towed behind a vehicle with a trailer hitch.

PRO TIP

If you order truck delivery of concrete, use the sales staff at the supplier as a resource. They can check your calculations for how much material to order and advise you about additives you might want. If you aren't certain that a mixer truck will have good access, request a site visit beforehand.

Paddle mixers consist of an eggbeater-type wand powered by a heavy-duty drill (as shown at right). They're the easiest way to prepare sand mixes and concrete resurfacing products. Pour most of the liquid into a bucket or tub with a capacity greater than the amount you are mixing. Add the dry ingredients. Then direct the paddle up and down into the mix.

Rental companies carry powerful, dedicated paddle mixers. For small batches of thin material, such as concrete resurfacers, you can fit a mixing paddle into a standard $\frac{1}{2}$-inch drill.

A Beginner's Strategy

If you are a beginner and want to tackle a path or patio, make the job easier by dividing the project into smaller sections and mixing the concrete yourself. Build a grid of permanent wood dividers from pressure-treated 2 × 4s rated for ground contact, or composite boards made of wood fiber and plastic. If sections are larger than 3 feet square, install interior 2 × 4 stakes, as shown. Drive 3-inch deck screws in partway to firmly anchor the concrete to the boards. Masking tape protects the wood from smears.

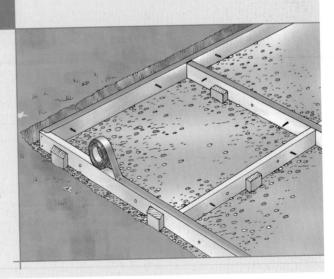

The recipes call for "parts" of various ingredients. Think of a part as a measuring cup that can change its size according to the scale of the project. A 5-gallon bucket makes a convenient measure, as it holds $^2/_3$ of a cubic foot.

BASIC CONCRETE MIX

$^1/_2$ part cement
1 part pea gravel ($^3/_8$ inch or less)
1 part sand
Approximately $^1/_4$ part water
Yield: about $1^1/_2$ parts concrete

BASIC SAND MIX

1 part cement
2 parts sand
Approximately $^1/_2$ part water
Yield: about 2 parts sand mix

Choosing a Scratch Recipe

There are literally hundreds of different formulas for concrete. But for projects like those in this book, two basic recipes work well. They differ primarily in the size of aggregate they contain. Basic Concrete Mix contains gravel, so it's suitable for projects such as paths, patios, and wall foundations. It needs to be poured more than 2 inches thick. Use Basic Sand Mix to make steppingstones $1^1/_2$ to 2 inches thick or to resurface old concrete with a layer 1 to 2 inches thick. The layer can be as thin as $^1/_2$ inch if you replace half of the mix water with acrylic or latex fortifier.

Varying the Basic Recipes

You can tweak the basic recipes in several ways:
- Add $^1/_2$ part more cement plus a little additional water to create a creamier cement. Benefit: produces a smoother finish with less effort.
- Replace up to half the water with acrylic or latex fortifier. Benefit: creates denser concrete that's less porous and less likely to crack. For sand mix: also allows applications $^1/_2$ to 1 inch thick.
- Add polypropylene fibers. Benefit: protects against surface cracks. For sand mix: also adds stiffness.
- Replace part of the cement (up to 15 percent) with fly ash or metakaolin and reduce the amount of water. Benefit: makes concrete denser, easier to shape, and less prone to surface cracks.

Safety

Cement is dusty when dry and caustic when damp, and cement mixtures often contain considerable quantities of crystalline silica, which can damage your lungs. Wear a disposable respirator (the two-elastic kind) when you work with dry ingredients. Whether you are handling dry mix or wet concrete, always wear rubber gloves. Add boots if you are pouring an object wider than you can reach across. Eye protection is smart too. When you're pouring concrete, check the top of your gloves and boots frequently for unnoticed spills that may cause blisters you won't feel at first. Rinse off any spills promptly.

Cement is about as caustic as lye, so it's crucial to pay attention to safety. You need a mask only when you are working with dry material, but you should wear gloves whether the mix is wet or dry.

CONCRETE STEPPINGSTONES

CASTING INDIVIDUAL STEPPING-STONES allows you to create a one-of-a-kind pathway without having to deal with a lot of concrete at once. The kidney shape of these steppingstones allows you to place the pieces close together to create a solid walkway if you wish.

1 **PREPARE THE MOLD.** With a jigsaw, cut the shape from ³/₄-inch-thick plywood. This mold is 25 inches long and about 14 inches wide. Cut two strips of aluminum flashing 2³/₄ inches wide to go around the perimeter (measure with string). Tape the layers together, then screw them to the plywood. Spray with shellac, let dry, and then spray with cooking oil and blot up the excess.

2 **ADD SAND MIX AND DECORATE.** Prepare Basic Sand Mix (see page 92) or a bagged sand mix. Fill the mold with it and scrape it level. Begin decorating immediately with damp pebbles set on edge. Tamp pieces level by covering them with a small piece of plywood and gently hammering straight down. With a trowel, work the surface cream of cement and fine sand over the stones.

3 **BRUSH THE SURFACE.** When the sand mix stiffens, brush off the surface to reveal the pebbles. Wipe with a sponge.

4 **BUILD THE PATH.** The next day, run a putty knife around the top edge to break the seal. Remove screws on the inward curve, then screw wooden handles to both ends. Invert the mold. Reuse the mold for additional steppingstones. Scrape off concrete residue and add more cooking oil each time. Install the steppingstones as shown on pages 36–37.

DECORATIVE CONCRETE PATH

THIS PATH IS DIVIDED INTO SHORT SECTIONS that were poured one at a time. Besides making the project more suitable for beginners, this strategy also solves a practical problem. The path is 4 inches thick, 9½ feet long, and 2 to 6½ feet wide, so it was too small to have concrete delivered from a truck and too large for a few people to mix and pour the concrete all at once. When the path was divided into thirds, a couple of batches in a 3.5-cubic-foot mixer filled each section.

1 **PREPARE THE SITE AND BUILD THE FORMS.** Mark the general outline of the path and excavate at least 6 inches to allow a slightly elevated 4-inch-thick slab over a 4-inch-thick bed of gravel. Dig a few inches deeper if you live where soil freezes. Add the gravel base and then build the form, or reverse these steps. If you are using a vibrating plate compactor to tamp the gravel, install the gravel first. If you are doing it by hand, you can build the form first. Build straight forms from 2 × 4s. For curved sections, use two layers of benderboard or a single layer of ⁷/₁₆-inch-thick composite siding (see page 48). Drive stakes no more than 3 feet apart along the outside and screw the edging to them. Slope the top at least ⅛ inch per foot (or ¼ inch per foot if the path is next to a building).

2 **CUT WIRE.** If you want to use chicken wire to stamp a design on the surface, cut pieces that fit within each section, minus a 2-inch perimeter. Remove the wire and place it on a lawn or another flat area. Weight the wire so it straightens.

3 **MAKE DECORATIVE INLAYS.** Make feather inlays or other designs from copper sheeting, which cuts almost as easily as wood. Wearing goggles, use a scroll saw or a coping saw with a fine-tooth blade. File the edges. Solder wire anchors to the backs. Clean off any flux residue.

4 **MIX THE CONCRETE AND SCREED IT LEVEL.** Prepare Basic Concrete Mix (see page 92) or a bagged concrete mix rich in cement, such as high-early-strength. Add pigment if you wish. As one person dumps the concrete into one end of the form and screeds (levels) it with a flat 2 × 4, another person should immediately begin mixing the next batch. Add each batch to the edge of concrete already poured, not in layers.

5 **ROUND THE EDGES AND SMOOTH THE SURFACE.** Run an edging tool around the perimeter to round over the edges. If rocks get in the way, seat them by pressing straight down with a margin trowel, as shown. Once water on the surface disappears, smooth the concrete with a wood or magnesium float. The surface should look uniform and fairly smooth, but it doesn't need to be perfect.

6 **EMBED THE INLAYS.** Press the cutouts into the concrete and wiggle them gently to help the concrete fill in around the anchor wires. It's better to seat the inlays a bit too deep than to risk having them sit above the surface.

7 **ADD TEXTURE.** When the surface is somewhat stiff but still pliable, set the chicken wire in place. With a trowel in each hand, press straight down. Repeat over the surface. Lift the wire and smooth the perimeter with the edging tool again.

8 **CLEAN THE INLAYS AND LET THE CONCRETE CURE.** As the concrete stiffens, wipe any excess from the inlays with a damp sponge. Remove the perimeter forms a day after you pour. Keep the concrete damp for at least three days.

CONCRETE PATIO

BUILDING A PATIO LARGE ENOUGH TO WARRANT ORDERING READY-MIX CONCRETE from a truck is an ambitious undertaking. And the larger the slab, the more ambitious the effort. The reward, though, is an amazing transformation of your yard in a short amount of time. You will need at least several reliable helpers. If you are pouring a patio larger than 100 square feet, or if you want a smooth finish on a smaller slab, consider hiring an experienced cement finisher to help. If you need a building permit, check on what inspections you need. Review pages 38–45 for details on laying out a project, excavating, adding gravel, and dealing with drainage.

Excavation and Edging

1 **EXCAVATE AND ADD GRAVEL.** With a shovel or small earth-moving machine, excavate for a gravel base at least 4 inches deep in mild climates, or at least 6 inches deep where soil freezes, plus $3^{1}/_{2}$ to 4 inches for concrete. Add the gravel (or half of it if you need more than 4 inches) and roughly level it with a garden rake turned upside down.

2 **COMPACT THE GRAVEL.** Maneuver a vibrating plate compactor over the gravel. Steering in a circular pattern, make three or four passes over each area. Measure down from the eventual top of the concrete. If the gap is more than 4 inches, add more gravel and compact the surface again.

3 **PREPARE CURVED EDGING.** Build the forms as you would construct wood edging (see pages 47–49). But if you plan to remove the forms, you don't need rot-resistant wood and you should anchor the stakes to the edging by driving screws from the outside, not the inside, of the form. To make an inexpensive curved edge, rip an 8-inch-wide plank of $^{7}/_{16}$-inch-thick manufactured siding in half, using the base of a circular saw as a guide. Use the smooth factory edge on the top of the form. If the curved edging is not long enough, splice two pieces by screwing them to a 6-foot-long backer piece. A short backer piece would result in an uneven curve.

4 **STAKE THE FORM.** At one corner of the form, drive stakes on both sides of the form material. Work your way along the edging, driving more stakes as you gradually push or pull the wood into the shape you want. Be careful not to make such a sharp bend that the wood snaps.

5 **TRANSITION TO STRAIGHT FORMS.**
Where a curve ends and a straight side begins, ensure a smooth transition by screwing the curved edging to the side of a stake, as shown. Then screw through the face of the stake into the end of the straight 2 × 4 edging. Drive a second stake immediately behind the first. Trim the first stake level with the edging. *continued* ▶▶

Add Screed Guides

Select a straight 2 × 4 to use as a screed for leveling the concrete. Check whether you can maneuver it across the forms in all areas. If one edge of the patio runs against the house, you won't have a guide edge. Snap a chalk line just above the finished height of the concrete and use that as a visual guide for the screed. If the screed isn't long enough to reach across the forms, stake a temporary screed guide where needed and make a note to remove it as soon as you have leveled the concrete so you can shovel in concrete to fill the gap.

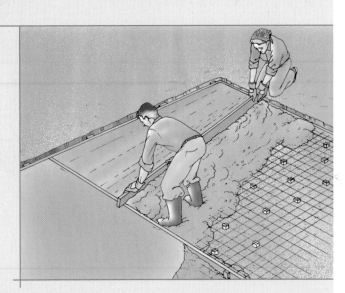

6 **CHECK THE SLOPE.** When forms are tentatively set, use a level on a long, straight board to check the slope. On this patio, the highest point of the paving needs to be the bottom of the lowest riser on steps leading from the house. Adjust the height of the forms if necessary. When you're satisfied, drive more stakes so there is at least one every few feet. If forms rise above the gravel base, add a lower level and hammer in diagonal bracing as shown.

7 **ADD REINFORCEMENT.** To keep the slab intact even if cracks develop, add 6-inch wire mesh or create a grid of ½-inch rebar. If you're using mesh that comes in a roll, unroll a length and then roll it backward to flatten it. Cut strands with lineman's pliers. For rebar, either rent a rebar cutter or cut partway through with a hacksaw or reciprocating saw and then bend the metal until the pieces break apart. Wire rebar intersections using a swivel tool made for the purpose. Elevate the rebar on stones or manufactured pieces known as chairs, or plan to pull up the rebar as you add concrete, which makes it easier to get wheelbarrows across the slab.

8 **PLAN FOR ACCESS.** Concrete should be placed where it will wind up, not scraped across the gravel base from one side of the patio to the other. To allow wheelbarrow access, remove a section of edging that you can reinstall just before you add the final load of concrete, or build a ramp.

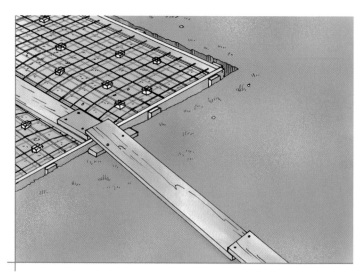

When New Concrete Meets Old

When a patio abuts the foundation of a house, it needs to be either tied into the existing concrete or isolated from it. Tying them together is a good approach where all the other edges of the patio are unconstrained. That way they can expand or contract or shift slightly in elevation as the weather changes. Where other edges are constrained or where the ground freezes deep, it's better to isolate the two sections.

To tie a new slab to a house, use a hammer drill with a carbide bit to bore ⅝-inch-diameter holes into the side of the foundation where rebar reinforcement will reach the slab. Slip the reinforcement into the holes.

To isolate a slab from a foundation, snap a chalk line on the foundation to indicate the height of the slab. Use construction adhesive to attach a strip of fibrous isolation joint to the house. Glue it firmly so it stays in place when you screed and finish the new concrete.

One Last Check

Read through all of the installation and finishing steps before the truck arrives, as you won't have time for this afterward.

- If you need a permit, have you scheduled the necessary inspections?

- Are helpers scheduled to arrive before the truck is due, and do they have appropriate safety gear, including impervious gloves and boots?

- Does each person have an assigned job? You may need two people to handle wheelbarrows and two or three people in the formed area to spread the concrete and screed it level. One of those people should direct traffic. Also assign jobs that need to be done once the concrete is in place, including smoothing the surface, dealing with any leftover concrete, and washing tools as each phase is completed.

- Are all tools on hand? You can rent what you don't own. Your list should include two heavy-duty wheelbarrows, several shovels, a bull float (or a darby if the slab is small), at least one magnesium or wood float, a screed board, a jointer, an edger, a broom, one or two kneeling boards, and perhaps a steel trowel. To keep the concrete from drying out too fast, you'll also need a liquid curing compound or enough plastic to cover the concrete.

- Are forms firm and properly sloped, and are any temporary screed guides or isolation joints in place?

- Is reinforcement at the right height, or have the people leveling the concrete been assigned to pull it up as the concrete is added?

- Have you tested the wheelbarrow paths by maneuvering a load of gravel over them?

WORK-SAVING TIP

If you wind up with excess concrete and haven't planned for a way to use it, shovel it into small piles that are easy to lift. Once the material hardens, bury the clods or take them to a landfill that recycles waste concrete.

1 **LOAD THE WHEELBARROW.** Set the wheelbarrow on a stable surface under the truck's chute. Orient it so it's headed toward the slab. If you have built a wooden path, have the wheel resting on the beginning of it so that you can take off smoothly. Ask the driver to load the first wheelbarrow only half full. You can increase the loads once you get used to the work. Scrape the chute after the concrete stops pouring out, so that none spills onto the ground.

2 **WHEEL AND POUR.** Wheel a load of concrete carefully; it's easy to spill if you have not practiced. If you start to lose control, don't try to right the wheelbarrow. Instead, push down on the handles with both hands. Then pick up the handles and start again. Wheel the concrete to a far corner of the formed area and dump the load.

Pouring and Smoothing

When the concrete truck arrives, check the consistency of the batch and ask the driver how long it will take to stiffen. If it's a hot day or the slab is very large, especially if you need to move the concrete in wheelbarrows, you might want a retarder added to give you more working time. Otherwise, a stiff mix without retarder is best.

3 **FILL THE FORMS.** The shovelers should spread the concrete until it is even with, or slightly above, the top of the form boards. Fill low spots, especially against the forms, with shovelfuls of concrete. Dump each load alongside previous ones.

4 **ADJUST THE REINFORCEMENT.** Make sure that the reinforcement is roughly in the middle of the concrete's thickness. Use a rake or a gloved hand to pull it up as needed. Tap the outside of the form boards to help the concrete settle snugly against the boards.

5 **SCREED THE CONCRETE.** As soon as a few wheelbarrow loads are in place, begin leveling the surface with the screed. Rest the ends on the forms or on a form and a temporary screed guide, or next to a chalk line if there is no edge form. Using a back-and-forth sawing motion, draw the screed across the surface to flatten the concrete to the same height as the forms.

7 **REMOVE THE SCREED GUIDE AND REINSTALL THE EDGING.** As you continue to add and level the concrete, take care not to close off your entry point into the form. If the slab is large enough to need a temporary screed guide, fill and screed the second section as you did the first. When both sections are filled, remove the guide. Fill the resulting trough with shovelfuls of concrete. If you removed a section of the form for wheelbarrow access, reinstall it before you add concrete to that area.

6 **FILL LOW SPOTS.** If there are voids when you screed, fill them by scattering concrete on the surface, then screed again. Don't plop in large amounts, as doing so could cause particles to separate unevenly.

Edges and Joints

With a few specialized tools, you can create nicely rounded edges and attractive control joints on concrete slabs.

To create the control joints that keep shrinkage cracks from forming (see page 89), you can divide the slab into sections with permanent wood edging, or wait until the concrete sets and then cut the joints with a circular saw fitted with a diamond blade. Or, while the concrete is still workable, set a straight 2 × 4 on top of it as a guide. Run a jointer back and forth several times until the concrete is smooth.

1. For the edge treatment, first slip a mason's trowel between the inside of the forms and the concrete, then slice all along the perimeter of the slab.

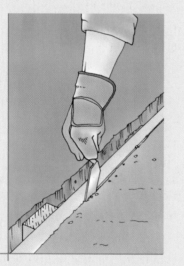

2. Then run an edging tool along the outside edges of the form and along both sides of any permanent wood dividers. It will take two or three passes to create a smooth edge.

Finishing the Concrete

How much finishing you need to do depends on what look you are trying to create. If you are planning to seed the surface with aggregate (see pages 110–111), skip the following steps except for rounding over edges and forming control joints. If you plan to stamp or stencil a design, apply a broom finish, or mortar brick or stone to the surface, smooth the concrete with a bull float or darby, attend to edges and joints, and you're ready to go. For a smooth finish, the most difficult effect for beginners to master, you'll need all of those steps plus troweling the surface. Note that ultra-smooth finishes become slippery when wet, so they aren't suitable for most walks and patios.

1 **SMOOTH WITH A BULL FLOAT OR DARBY.** If you are working on a large slab, smooth the surface with a bull float. Push the blade forward with the front edge slightly raised. Pull the tool back over the same territory to help push stones down and fill in small holes. After each back-and-forth stroke, lift the tool and move it over to create a parallel stroke. If the slab is small enough that you can reach across it, you can use a darby (a long wooden trowel) instead of a bull float. Make sweeping strokes. In either case, overlap strokes slightly so you float the entire surface.

2 **FLOAT THE SURFACE.** Initial floating causes water to rise to the surface. As soon as it disappears, run a magnesium or wood float over the surface. (A magnesium float is easier to use and is definitely recommended for beginners.) Hold the tool so that the leading edge is slightly raised and press down gently as you work. If you cannot reach across the slab, use a float on a pole or place a piece of plywood or foam insulation about 3 × 4 feet on the concrete and kneel on it. Start floating at the far corner and work back so that you do not kneel on newly floated concrete. You may need two work platforms so you can step them across the slab.

3 **TROWEL FINISH.** If you want a smooth surface (which might be too slippery for outdoor paving), again wait for any water on the surface to disappear. Then go over the concrete with a steel trowel. A pool trowel, which has rounded ends, is the easiest type for beginners to use, because there are no corners to dig into the surface. Hold the leading edge up and press down harder than you did with the magnesium float. The stiffer the concrete, the harder you must press.

The longer concrete stays damp after it's poured, the stronger it will be. Three days is a good minimum, and a week is even better. There is some benefit even at 28 days. In dry weather, mist the surface several times a day and keep it covered the rest of the time with damp cardboard or plastic. Or apply a curing compound, especially if you added pigment. These compounds prevent stains that can appear on tinted concrete if it dries unevenly.

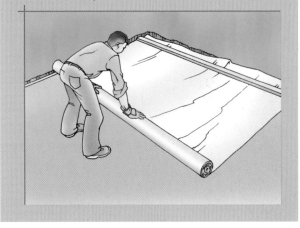

4 **BROOM FINISH.** For most outdoor paving, a slightly rough surface is better. Skip step 3 and instead gently drag a push broom across the floated surface. Pull it, don't push. The stiffer the broom bristles, the more pronounced the texture will be. If the bristles are not digging in and producing the surface you like, try wetting the broom. Work carefully and aim to produce a consistent texture with straight lines. Avoid overlapping the strokes; they should be right next to each other. Clean the broom immediately after use.

DECORATIVE EFFECTS

IF YOU DON'T LIKE THE LOOK OF STANDARD CON-CRETE, transform it by choosing a decorative effect. Add pigment to the mix, a simple change, or go for a more complex process that leaves the concrete textured and colored so that it resembles stone or other masonry materials. Besides using these techniques on the surface of freshly poured concrete before it sets, you can use many of them to decorate thin overlays that you apply to new or old concrete.

The varied colors in this path were created with several tones of color hardener spread onto freshly poured concrete. The grout lines look realistic because they were cut out with a grinder and filled with mortar. The mortar is shallow and has solid concrete underneath, so weeds won't take root as they might in sand joints between true flagstones.

Coloring Concrete

The most reliable way to achieve consistent color is to tint the concrete while it is mixing, known as integral color. Mixer trucks typically add a bag of pigment that dissolves in the mixer. If you're mixing the concrete yourself, use liquid or dry pigment commonly sold at home centers for tinting up to two bags of concrete mix. Or, for a wider range of colors, buy dry pigment by the pound at a concrete-supply company. If you mix the concrete yourself, take care to measure all ingredients—even water—precisely to attain consistent color. For the brightest colors, use white cement, not the standard gray.

You can also apply pigment to the surface after you have leveled and bull-floated the concrete, as shown with the stenciling technique on page 108. For this, use a readymade color hardener or prepare a homemade equivalent of dry pigment, cement, and fine sand in a 1:6:6 ratio. Applying pigment just to the surface saves money because you use less pigment, but the color is more varied.

Stains are another way to add color to concrete. Acid stains react with ingredients in the hardened concrete and result in mottled color permanently bonded to the surface. The "acid" in the name refers to hydrochloric acid, which etches the surface so mineral salts in the formulas can react with hydrated lime in the concrete. Because of the acid, you'll need to follow the manufacturer's safety instructions precisely. Water-based and solvent-based stains for concrete are also available.

Tooling In a Design

This decorative touch is easiest to create on a path that you can reach across. A flagstone design looks best if the concrete is tinted or if it is stained after it has cured. Using several colors looks most realistic. Begin this technique after you have floated the surface with a bull float or a darby, edged the perimeter, and floated a second time with a magnesium float.

1 **TOOL THE SURFACE.** With a convex jointer made for striking joints on a brick wall, press a design into the surface. Pull the tool toward you. For a flagstone look, aim to distribute small and large sizes throughout the slab.

2 **TROWEL OVER THE PATTERN.** With a magnesium float or a steel trowel, go over the surface to knock down most of the crumbs and any exposed gravel.

3 **BRUSH THE SURFACE.** If you are working on a relatively small area, use a paintbrush or a mason's brush to gently clear away any remaining crumbs and to produce a finely textured broom finish over the entire surface. On a long path on a hot day, skip this step; the concrete could harden too much before you texture the entire surface.

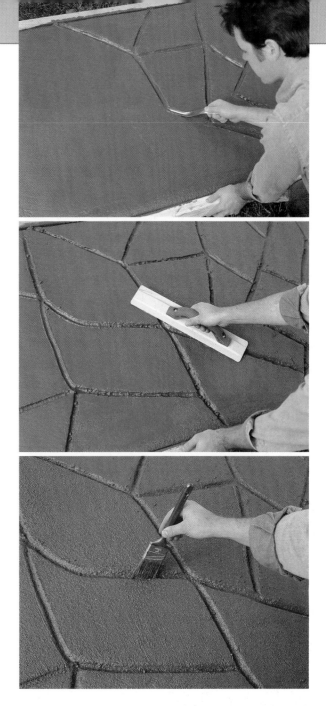

Other Options

If you don't want to make concrete mimic stone but still want to add texture and interest to a path, consider tooling a geometric design or free-form pattern into the surface. If the design incorporates straight lines, place a board on the surface and trace against the edge.

Besides tooling a design into freshly poured concrete, you can top old concrete with a layer of sand mix and tool the design into that. Coat the old concrete first with bonding adhesive, and replace part of the mix water with more bonding adhesive if the new layer will be less than 1 inch thick.

This design was tooled into Basic Sand Mix (see page 92) prepared with white cement and yellow pigment. The mix was applied as a topping to a concrete paver.

Stamping Concrete

Stamping a design is simple in concept, not all that different from pressing a hand into damp concrete. Just set down textured mats, tamp on the back, and peel them off to reveal the design. But there can be complications, such as spaces where mats don't fit. You may want to hire a professional finisher with experience in stamping. Stamping a large patio requires a crew of skilled workers.

Supplies for this job are available at concrete-supply companies rather than home centers. Show a drawing of your job to the salesperson to make sure you get all the tools you need. Most mats butt against each other to create a continuous pattern, so you should have at least two or three mats, which you may be able to rent. Seamless mats, however, can overlap and so can be used in no particular order. You may need a special flexible mat for hard-to-reach places and edges, and perhaps an old chisel to create lines where even these mats cannot reach. There are also edging stamps to create the look of brick or stone edging. Be sure to get a hand tamper as well.

The same store probably sells pigment that you can incorporate into the concrete as you mix it. Color isn't essential, but it adds to the look. You also need a bucket of powdered release agent, which keeps the mats from sticking. The release agent affects the color, so ask the supplier for a picture of the final appearance.

Before you pour the concrete, measure and mark the forms so you know the best place to begin stamping. After pouring, screed the concrete, float it with a bull float or a darby, edge the corners, and smooth the surface with a magnesium float. Then you're ready to stamp.

Other Stamped Designs

Besides using textured mats that simulate stone or brick, you can stamp concrete with other materials. Use nonabsorbent objects with simple shapes.

These concrete tiles were cast like steppingstones (see page 93) and then stamped with the bottoms of plastic drinking cups. For thin tiles, like these 1/2- to 3/4-inch-thick pieces, use a sand mix and replace half the water with concrete bonding adhesive.

1 **APPLY THE RELEASE AGENT.** As soon as the bleed water from floating disappears, broadcast the release agent over the surface at the rate recommended on the label. Make sure the entire surface is coated. Release agent contains cement, so it's a good idea to wear gloves as you do this step.

2 **POSITION AND STAMP THE MATS.** Carefully align the first two or three mats so they are precisely positioned. A slight error will be multiplied as you impress additional mats. Once you are sure of the alignment, walk on the mats and use a hand tamper to press them all the way down.

3 **CONTINUE STAMPING.** Work rapidly so that the concrete does not have time to harden. As soon as a set of mats has been stamped, pick up each mat and lay it again. Always have at least two mats in position so that it is easy to butt new mats against them. If the concrete does start to harden, you may need to pound the mats with a rubber mallet. You may also need to touch up some joints by tapping with a chisel.

4 **PRESSURE-WASH AND SEAL.** Cover the concrete with plastic. After a day or two, when the concrete has started to cure, spray the surface with a pressure washer. Use a fan nozzle held about 2 feet above the surface and move it evenly and slowly. This will remove excess release agent and will reveal darker and lighter lines that heighten the textured appearance. Replace the plastic and allow the concrete to cure for a week or so. Once the concrete is fully cured, apply sealer.

Stenciling a Design

With paper stencils, textured rollers, and a mixture of cement, fine sand, and pigment that you trowel into the surface, you can create a look similar to that of stamped concrete but in a way that offers several advantages. With a few scissor snips, you can modify the stencils to avoid the awkward shapes that sometimes result from stamping. You can also make apparent grout lines in the design line up with control joints needed to prevent cracks. Pour the concrete and go over it with a bull float or a darby. Round over the edges if you wish. Then you're ready to begin stenciling. The steps aren't difficult, but have plenty of help on hand.

1 **PLACE BORDER STENCILS.** This design includes a ribbon of small squares around the edges, which are adapted with scissors to follow the curved edge. The border stencils also go across the slab in the two places where control joints will be cut in a few days. As the stencils are placed, they're gently smoothed down with a finger so all edges adhere to the damp surface.

2 **SPREAD FIELD STENCILS.** Field stencils come in long rolls about 3 feet wide and have ragged edges that interlock. To keep a long length airborne until it is in the right position, a helper in the center lifts the middle of the stencil with a pole. To smooth stencils far from the edge, the crew uses a pool trowel on a pole.

3 **BROADCAST COLOR HARDENER.** When all of the stencils are in place and pressed to the surface, a product known as color hardener is broadcast over the surface. The material consists of cement, pigment, and fine sand, so it acts as a topping layer that gets all its moisture from the underlying concrete. Apply different colors to some sections if you want.

4 **WORK IN THE TOPPING.** With a magnesium float, press down on the topping and incorporate it into the top of the slab. Use short strokes and take care not to lift the stencils. Once all of the topping is moist, move on to the next section.

5 **EXTEND YOUR REACH.** You have a couple of options for working in the topping in the middle of a large area. The man on the left is using a pole with a pool float, which looks like a big trowel but has rounded ends. You can also work from a plank, available at tool-rental companies, that's held aloft by supports just outside the forms. Working on a support board (see step 2, page 103) is a third option.

6 **APPLY MORE TOPPING.** Broadcast a second coat of color hardener over the surface and work it in. Toss handfuls of release agent over the surface until it's completely covered. The surface material has the consistency of talcum powder, so work upwind or wear a respirator so you don't inhale the dust.

7 **TEXTURE THE SURFACE.** Go over the surface in several directions with textured rollers, which you can rent. A small edging roller is good for curves. In the middle of the concrete, use a larger roller and wear textured pads over your boots.

8 **REMOVE THE STENCILS.** When you're done adding the texture, pull up the stencils. This is an exciting step because you see the design for the first time. Leave the release agent in place for a couple of days. Meanwhile, keep the slab covered with plastic if the weather is dry or hot. Then rinse with a pressure washer. Use a fan nozzle held about 2 feet above the surface. Cut control joints with a diamond blade in a circular saw. Re-cover the concrete and keep it moist for another few days.

9 **THE FINAL RESULT.** Areas covered by the stencils didn't pick up any pigment, so they are still gray. They also didn't get any additional cement or sand, so they are about $^1/_8$ inch lower than the colored sections.

Seeding Aggregate

There are two ways to create an exposed-aggregate surface. You can pour standard concrete but apply a retarder to the surface so the concrete there doesn't set well. Then you brush that away and reveal some of the gravel that normally lies hidden beneath the surface. The other method, shown here, involves scattering pebbles on the surface and working them in enough to become locked in yet still visible. Many people prefer this approach so they can select pebbles that are especially beautiful and pay for only the ones they'll see.

Ready-mix-concrete companies carry decorative aggregate, as do some landscaping-supply companies. Companies that specialize in selling decorative concrete carry an even wider selection. Colors often run from brown to light tan. For more interest, consider adding pebbles of another color, such as black or red. Buy more aggregate than you think you'll need. You'll really be stuck if you run short.

This process takes longer than a standard broom finish, so unless you are working in a very small area, arrange for a retarder to be added to the concrete so you'll have extra time to work.

1 **SCATTER THE AGGREGATE.** Pour and screed the concrete. You do not need to float it, but make sure that all voids are filled and that the surface is flat and even. As soon as the bleed water has disappeared, use a shovel or your hands to scatter damp aggregate over the entire surface, aiming for a single layer. You may choose to sprinkle the area with colorful stones and perhaps even install several decorative accent stones.

2 **EMBED THE AGGREGATE.** Use a flat board to press the stones gently into the concrete. Rest both ends of the board on the edging to ensure that it does not press down and create a dent. If pressing the board down with your hand does not embed the stones, walk on the board.

3 **FLOAT OVER THE AGGREGATE.** If the slab is large, cover part of it with plastic to keep it wet until you reach that part, or assign helpers to different sections, as the concrete can harden even if it is covered. Work the surface with a magnesium float so that a thin layer of cement without any gravel in it works its way up and barely covers the aggregate stones. Avoid overworking the surface, and produce as little bleed water as possible. Use an edger to round off the perimeter.

④ BRUSH AND SPRAY. When the concrete has begun to harden, spray a fine mist over a small area where you troweled first, then brush away the top layer using a broom or a mason's brush. Stop once the tops of the aggregate are exposed. If stones start coming loose, wait for the concrete to harden further before you move on to brushing and spraying the rest of the slab. Allow the slab to cure slowly by keeping it damp for at least three days. Cover it with plastic if the weather is hot or dry. If a haze is present after the concrete is fully cured, wash the surface with a concrete cleaner.

Travertine Finish

This finish, which is suitable only where temperatures don't dip below freezing, produces an effect similar to a knock-down stucco finish. If you color the finish mixture so that it contrasts with the underlying concrete, the effect will be heightened.

Pour, screed, and float the surface with a darby or bull float, followed by a magnesium or wood float. Use an edging tool to round off the perimeter.

① MIX AND APPLY TEXTURE. In a bucket, dry-mix one part portland cement with 2 parts sand. Add just enough water to produce a stiff mix. Wait for water on top to disappear, then dip a mason's brush into the mixture and dash it all over the concrete. If the mixture sinks in, wait for the concrete to become a bit harder. Produce blotches of various sizes, but aim to have an even mix of large and small blotches throughout the slab.

② KNOCK DOWN HIGH SPOTS. Wait until the mixture has started to harden, perhaps about half an hour. Gently scrape the surface with a steel trowel held nearly flat, using long, sweeping strokes. The resulting texture will be fairly smooth on the high spots and rougher in the low spots.

RESURFACING CONCRETE

A GROWING NUMBER OF PRODUCTS MAKE IT POSSIBLE TO COVER DRAB OR STAINED CONCRETE with a fresh layer that can be tinted or textured to create decorative effects. Once available only to professionals, many of these products now are sold to homeowners as well. Options include micro toppings, which are only $1/16$ to $1/8$ inch thick; stamp overlays, which are $1/4$ to $1/2$ inch thick, depending on the stamp that will be used; and self-leveling overlays, which can be $1/4$ to 2 inches thick, enough to level and smooth out a damaged surface. The formulas all consist of cement, sand or other aggregate, and polymer, a broad category that includes white glue and a virtually equivalent adhesive sold as concrete bonding agent. The specific polymers in overlays are one of the main things that distinguish one product from the next.

Instead of troweling edges square when you apply a resurfacing product, you can install simple forms made with 2 × 2s or 2 × 4s butted against the existing slab. Stake the forms slightly higher than the slab and spread the material to the edges.

Basic resurfacing mixes that result in overlays $1/4$ to $3/8$ inch thick are sold by the bag at home centers. These products are durable, and they can be tinted with standard concrete pigments. But because the mixes tend to incorporate gray cement, the resulting colors will be muted.

Clean the old concrete and patch any cracks. Plan the pour for a time when the sun won't be shining directly on the surface. Using a paddle mixer in a drill, mix the resurfacer with water to produce a paste that is just thin enough to pour. You will need to work fairly quickly. Spread it at a uniform thickness, using a magnesium float or a broom-handled squeegee. Do not feather the edges, as thin edges can chip off. Troweling the material to a square edge is a better solution.

Homemade knee boards allow you to trowel resurfacing material onto a slab that is too wide to reach across. Screw tips protrude on the back, so the boards leave only pinhole marks in the topping. As you work your way out of the slab, trowel over these marks to make them disappear.

A gauge roller has ridges that automatically spread thin cement-based overlays to a specified thickness.

Specialty resurfacing products often incorporate white cement, so you can tint them to produce brilliant colors. Follow label instructions about mixing and finishing. You will probably need a paddle mixer in a drill, as well as a gauge roller (see opposite page, bottom right) or a gauge rake to spread the overlay to the recommended depth. As the topping stiffens, you can trowel it smooth, press in texture, cut simulated grout lines, or create other decorative effects.

You can create the look of stone with a basic concrete resurfacing mix tinted brown. Spread the material with a squeegee and wait for the topping to stiffen. Kneeling on homemade knee boards, scratch the design with a cut-off nail. As the topping stiffens, use a soft cloth to buff the surface and work debris from the scratches back into the lines. It will harden there and resemble grout.

To color concrete overlays, you can add pigment to the mix or rub in stains after the material has cured. To create the look of tiles, score lines with an angle grinder.

Resurfacing with Sand Mix

You can make your own topping mix from Basic Sand Mix (see page 92) or use a bagged sand mix. If you add only water, spread the material 1 to 2 inches thick. For a layer as thin as 1/2 inch, replace half the usual water with concrete bonding agent.

Clean old concrete and patch any cracks. Build forms from 2 × 2s or 2 × 4s, staked to create the gap that you want to fill. Brush a coat of bonding adhesive over the concrete and wait until the liquid becomes tacky (or to the stage recommended on the label). Prepare the sand mix, add it to the form, screed it level with a straight board long enough to reach across the form, and finish the surface as you would if it were new concrete. A broom finish, a stencil design, and even an exposed-aggregate surface are all options. If you use exposed aggregate, install a thick enough layer of sand mix so the pebbles account for no more than one-fifth of the thickness.

A topping made from bagged sand mix gives old concrete a new look. This topping was spread and leveled; then sprinkled with a mixture of dry pigment, cement, and fine sand in a 1:6:6 ratio; and troweled. The final finish was created with a broom dragged in curves. Then the perimeter was smoothed with an edging tool.

garden walls

GARDEN WALLS HELP DEFINE OUTDOOR SPACES AND GIVE ORDER TO A LANDSCAPE. THEY ALSO HAVE PRACTICAL BENEFITS, SUCH AS PROVIDING PRIVACY, ACTING AS A WINDBREAK, AND HOLDING BACK SOIL TO STOP EROSION OR MAKE GARDENING EASIER. WALLS COVERED WITH BRICK, STONE, OR STUCCO ALSO LOOK GREAT, AND THEY ARE VIRTUALLY MAINTENANCE FREE, PROVIDED THEY ARE BUILT CORRECTLY. THIS CHAPTER GIVES DESIGN IDEAS AND SHOWS HOW TO BUILD DIFFERENT TYPES OF WALLS.

CHOOSING A WALL STYLE

WALLS ADD A POWERFUL SENSE OF SHELTER to a garden. They make large or open gardens seem more intimate, and they work the same magic on small gardens when they screen out street noise or block views from the street. Brick, stone, and textured concrete blocks also create a pleasant contrast to leaves and flowers, making the plants look more lush. The materials you choose, as well as the way you assemble them, go a long way toward making your garden look tidy and formal or relaxed and rustic, or something in between.

ABOVE: Pillow-shaped stones form a low retaining wall in this garden, allowing a sloped area to be divided into two relatively flat spaces. The wall farther back is poured concrete. You can still see the impressions left by the boards used for forms.

LEFT: In this garden, concrete chunks, many of which still carry a coat of paint from their former life, appear as wall material, steps, and even edging. The edges reveal stones in the concrete mix, a look that's echoed in the gravel paving. In the wall, small chunks of concrete were used to stabilize the larger pieces and bring the top edge to a uniform level.

LEFT: Elegant in their simplicity, dry-stacked walls consist of stone and nothing else. Held together by gravity, they gain a lot of strength when topped by large, heavy cap-stones. By straddling numerous smaller pieces, these larger pieces anchor the stones underneath.

Designed for privacy and security, a tall brick wall steps down toward a pool, jutting in and out to provide seating and planting areas. This keeps the wall from seeming massive and intimidating. Instead, it looks human-scale and friendly—at least from the inside.

ABOVE: Stucco walls can work almost like sculptural elements in a garden. Tinted pink, this low wall serves as a decorative accent, frames the patio, and provides extra seating. Stucco walls usually have standard concrete blocks as a base.

BELOW: Stackable retaining blocks make wall building quick and relatively easy because pieces come in set sizes and are shaped so that they automatically interlock and step back a retaining wall at the right rate. A few styles can be used to make low walls that rise straight up, and some can even form freestanding walls. Suppliers can point you to products that will fit your needs.

ABOVE: Small, round rocks are one of the most difficult materials to use for building stable walls. But long-lasting results are possible, particularly if the wall is low and not where someone might climb on it. The wall needs to have good batter, meaning it must lean back into the slope.

BELOW: Where large capstones aren't an option, a mortared-together capstone layer also works well. The solid surface sheds water, which is especially important in areas where freezing temperatures are common. Ice within the wall could push the stones apart.

Designing a Wall

Garden walls break into two broad categories: freestanding walls, which have two exposed sides, and retaining walls, which literally rise from the soil and have just one face. Within each category, there are dry-stacked walls, whose parts are held in place with gravity alone, and mortared walls, which are glued together with a sand-and-cement mixture. Deciding which features you want involves practical issues as well as aesthetic considerations.

Dry-stacked walls need to be wider at the base (at least 2 feet for freestanding walls built of stone), but they don't need much in the way of a foundation. If you plan to build the wall yourself or with helpers who are relatively inexperienced, this is usually the best option.

Mortared walls can be narrower, thus saving space. But they need substantial foundations where soil freezes deeply, and they usually require more expert labor. When they surround planting beds, low mortared walls look tidier than dry-stack walls because weeds aren't as likely to take root in the spaces. The mortar also helps keep wall materials in place, which is why walls built of small pieces, such as brick, are always built this way.

Before you settle on a design, ask at your local planning office whether you need a permit and, if so, what the requirements are. If you live where earthquakes are a concern, or if you want a tall wall or a tall retaining wall, a veneered wall might be your best option because reinforcement can be added to the core structure. The veneer topping can take on any look you want: stone or brick, mortared or dry-stacked.

Sloping Walls

Although retaining walls stay intact even if they have a gentle slope, designs that feature rectangular stones or blocks often look best when they stair-step down in level sections. Begin building these walls from the bottom of the slope. Excavate a level pad for each section. Lay level courses on the lowest section until each course becomes the foundation layer of the next section. This means the bottom stones will appear to rise gradually from the ground. Lay middle courses as if the wall were all one height. End sections at the appropriate heights.

LEFT: Adding mortar makes a low river-rock retaining wall more stable, provided the mortar is used on pieces that already fit together reasonably well.

RETAINING WALLS

RETAINING WALLS ARE COMMON ON HILLSIDE LOTS, where they hold back the slope or create terraces. But retaining walls also have a role on flat lots. A low retaining wall filled in behind with soil becomes a raised planting bed.

If you have a steep slope or an erosion problem, consult a landscape architect or soils engineer before you build. Many communities require a soils engineer to sign off on plans for retaining walls above a certain height—often 4 feet. Terraced walls and situations in which a driveway is above the wall also call for special review.

Excavating for a Retaining Wall

Most retaining walls batter, meaning they lean back toward the soil they retain. More step-back is better, up to a point. A 45-degree angle, where the step-back is equal to the height of the wall, gives maximum strength. But a wall slanted that much doesn't seem like much of a wall, and it defeats one purpose of most retaining walls, which is to create more useable flat space.

In most cases, before you begin building, you will need to excavate to create the rough shape you want. For a big job, consider bringing in a small earth-moving machine. There are three basic excavation strategies. One is to cut into the entire face of the hillside at roughly the same angle as the wall will batter. This will mean hauling away plenty of soil. The second option is to build the retaining wall at the bottom of the slope and then fill behind it with gravel and soil. This means hauling in lots of soil. The third option combines the first two and keeps soil hauling to a minimum: Excavate the bottom half of the slope and use the excavated soil to fill in the upper half. As you excavate, be sure to leave room for drainage gravel if needed.

For maximum strength, a dry-stacked stone retaining wall needs to slope in two directions. The face of the wall must batter, or lean back into the slope it retains, and the top course must also slant slightly toward the slope. The high point should be the outward edge of the rim. This wall incorporates both features.

Stacked-Block Wall

The easiest retaining walls to build consist of stackable concrete retaining blocks. The pieces come in set sizes, and they usually interlock in a way that automatically steps back the wall by the correct amount from one course to the next. Choose a style with a rough front face if you want the wall to resemble stone. If you want greenery to eventually cover the wall, choose blocks with a hollow center for soil and plants.

Block designs vary, so read the manufacturer's installation instructions. Some blocks have lips, while others fit together with grooves or with fiberglass pins. Styles that allow you to build walls with no batter may need to be shorter than sloped walls, even if the materials are the same.

Installation is straightforward. If you want a straight wall, string mason's twine to mark the front edge. Dig a trench big enough so that you can install a 6-inch base of compacted gravel under the first course and have 6 to 8 inches of gravel behind the blocks, or whatever the manufacturer recommends. Compact the base with a vibrating plate compactor, if possible, or use a hand tamper. If you want a level wall, check that the base is level. A gentle slope won't affect the wall's strength, though.

Lay the foundation row of blocks. If the blocks have lips, set the bottom row of blocks upside down and backward. Adjust the blocks by adding or removing gravel so they form an even surface and do not wobble. Add drain pipe as needed.

Lay the second row of blocks. Stagger the joints in a running bond pattern. Backfill the space behind the wall with gravel, then tamp the gravel firm. Place subsequent rows of blocks in the same manner. Backfill and compact the gravel after each row. When you're near the top, lay landscaping fabric over the gravel and backfill the rest of the way with topsoil.

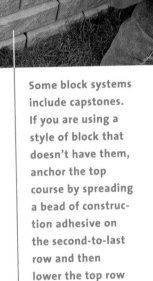

Some block systems include capstones. If you are using a style of block that doesn't have them, anchor the top course by spreading a bead of construction adhesive on the second-to-last row and then lower the top row onto that.

Improving Drainage

Water always moves downhill through the path of least resistance. To reduce the amount of water that will dribble through a retaining wall in wet weather, give it an easier route, through perforated drainpipe. Slope the pipe downhill to where you want the water to empty (see pages 44–45). Then build the wall as usual. Fill around the pipe with gravel. (If you are using landscaping cloth, drape it across the excavation and up the slope before you add the pipe, and fold the cloth over the top of the gravel.)

Flexible, corrugated drainpipe is easiest to use. Before you place the first course, set the pipe, with the holes pointed down, toward the back of the excavation.

Stacked Stones

A simple strategy results in a strong dry-stacked wall: Put two stones over one, and one over two. If you're building with irregular stone, you won't always be able to do this, but if you aim for it with every stone you place, a strong wall will usually result. Dry-stacked stone retaining walls must slope toward the soil they retain, usually by about ½ to 1 inch per foot.

1 **PREPARE THE SITE.** Excavate to attain roughly the slope you want and to create a depression several inches deep along the base of the wall. Nearby, set out stones for the first course; they should be the largest pieces you have. Place each with its flattest, widest face up so you can easily select the piece you want. Also stockpile drainage gravel nearby, using pieces of uniform size (without "fines" or small particles). Install drainage pipe if needed. Drive stakes every few feet to establish the approximate front face of the wall.

2 **SET THE BASE COURSE.** Place the foundation stones in the shallow excavation and align the front face with the line established by the stakes. Set pieces so they nest well together. If you need to raise an edge, or even an entire stone, fill in with gravel, not soil. You may need to try several pieces to find a good fit. Take the time, as the entire wall rests on this layer.

3 **CHECK ALIGNMENT AND ADD GRAVEL.** When all the foundation stones are in place, step back and check that the front faces create a straight line or one that curves smoothly, depending on the wall shape you want. Make any adjustments. Then fill in behind the foundation stones with gravel and add drainage pipe if needed. From the back, pack the gravel into crevices between the foundation stones. (If the soil is heavy clay, drape landscaping cloth over the slope first so the soil doesn't work its way into the gravel and clog it.)

4 **ADD LAYERS.** Continue adding gravel until it's level with the tops of the foundation stones. Then, starting at the ends or corners and working toward the middle, add a second course, then a third. If you place several small stones on one layer, try to bridge them with a bigger stone on the next course. To keep pieces from wobbling, tap chinking (small stones used as wedges) into the wall from the front or the back. Fill in behind with gravel as you go.

5 **SWITCH TO SOIL FILL.** As you near the top of the wall, stop adding gravel backfill. Tuck the landscaping cloth, if you are using it, over the top of the gravel and bend it up against the back of the stones. Fill the final inches with soil. Pack it in firmly.

6 **ADD THE TOP LAYER.** This wall has no capstones, but for a tidy look, it still needs a straight top edge. To create a reference line, stake mason's twine at the height you want. Then find stones that are as flat as possible on top and that fit well against adjoining stones.

7 **THE END RESULT.** The completed wall has stones that are level on top. They slant slightly toward the slope.

FREE-STANDING WALLS

EVEN THOUGH THEY LACK MORTAR, freestanding, dry-stacked stone walls can be amazingly durable. Many have lasted for centuries with little maintenance. The key is in the stacking.

Allow yourself plenty of time to experiment with different stones and different orientations, so that each stone rests solidly in the finished wall.

A stone wall calls for plenty of heavy lifting, so work with caution. Avoid stones that weigh more than 50 pounds, unless you are working with a helper. Have the stones delivered as close to the site as possible, and take periodic breaks. See pages 26–27 for tips on how to move stones safely and efficiently.

Choose stones that are at least partially squared off and flat on two sides, if possible. You will need tie stones, also called bond stones, long enough to span the thickness of the wall, or at least reach much of the way through it. Sort the stones into three or four piles according to size, reserving the largest, flattest pieces for the wall's cap.

A simple batter gauge (see page 122) helps you quickly ascertain that the sides of the wall lean inward.

A freestanding, dry-stacked stone wall gets its strength from its structure. Basically, it's a double retaining wall. Instead of battering into a slope, each side presses into the other and keeps the wall upright. The wall must always be wider at the base than at the top.

Setting Gate Pins

If you want to attach a gate to a stone wall that is either dry-laid or set in mortar, purchase a strap-and-pin hinge. Install the hinge pins first. When the stones reach the height of the lower hinge, leave a space several inches wide. Mix and spread type N or S mortar, set the pin in the mortar, and check that the pin is plumb. Allow the mortar to set before you build on top of that layer. Ensure the wall end is plumb as you build it up, and install the upper hinge in the same way. Then build the gate and attach the strap portions of the hinges to fit.

1 **DIG A TRENCH AND LAY THE FIRST STONES.** Remove sod and all other organic material from an area about 3 inches wider than the bottom perimeter of the wall. Scrape, rather than dig, the bottom of the excavation so that the stones will rest on undisturbed (still compacted) soil. If the site is not level, you may prefer to excavate a level area, in which case the bottom course of the finished wall will appear to disappear gradually into the ground. Otherwise, follow the slope of the yard and build a wall that is slightly out of level.

Lay a tie stone at each end of the wall, as well as every 6 to 8 feet along its length. For this course, place the flattest side up. Excavate underneath or add gravel as needed so the stones seat firmly. Fill in with stones laid in two wythes. Fill the spaces between the wythes with tightly packed stones.

CONSTRUCTION TIP

Interconnect the front and back of the wall by placing tie pieces at both ends and every 6 to 8 feet along the wall's length. The spacing depends on the size of the stones you are using. If possible, use tie stones that span the wall's width. Otherwise, select pairs of stones that each reach three-fourths of the way through. Set them so they project inward from opposite sides and butt tightly.

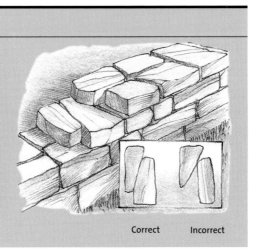

Correct   Incorrect

2 **LAY ADDITIONAL COURSES.** As you continue to lay stones, keep the courses fairly even. Set large stones on each side and fill in the middle with small stones where needed. To ensure a stable wall, always lay one on top of two rather than stack stones of the same size directly on top of each other. Use the batter gauge to check that the wall leans slightly inward on both sides. Every few courses, add tie stones. If you need to cut stones, see pages 28–29.

3 **FINISH THE WALL.** Fill gaps in the side of the wall by gently tapping in small stones. Take care not to dislodge larger stones. Also add stones as chinking to keep pieces from wobbling. Finish the top with large, flat capstones that overhang the sides of the wall. Test that the capstones are fairly stable when rested on top. Make any necessary adjustments, then mix a batch of mortar and lay a 1- to 2-inch-thick bed. Press the capstones into the mortar.

CONCRETE FOOTINGS

MOST MORTARED WALLS NEED A CONCRETE FOOTING, in contrast to a dry-laid wall's base of compacted gravel or even soil. A typical footing is 8 to 12 inches deep and twice as wide as the wall it will support. However, if the ground freezes where you live, local building codes may require a footing that extends below the frost line—the depth at which soil freezes in your area. In some locales, this may mean digging and pouring a footing that is 4 feet deep. If the footing will support only a modest garden wall, your inspector may allow a shallower footing that floats, meaning that it will rise and fall slightly when the ground freezes and thaws. Where winters are mild, you may even be able to use compacted gravel as a foundation (see page 130).

> **LABOR-SAVING TIP**
>
> If a footing needs to be quite deep, hire someone with a trenching machine or backhoe to dig a trench and then fill all but the top few inches with concrete.

If the footing will abut an existing structure, install a fibrous isolation joint (see page 99) to ensure that the new footing will not affect the existing structure if the footing rises or falls. In the method shown on these pages, the walls of a carefully dug trench act as the form for the concrete—except at the top, where 2 × 4s are used.

1 **LAY OUT AND DIG THE HOLE.** Use mason's line and wood stakes to lay out the outside perimeter of the 2 × 4 frame that will go on top (step 2). If the wall is to turn a corner, check for square. Dig the hole with a square-bladed shovel. The top three inches of the hole should be 1½ inches wider in all directions than the main hole, to accommodate the frame. Scrape, rather than dig, the bottom of the excavation and remove all loose soil so that the concrete will rest on undisturbed soil.

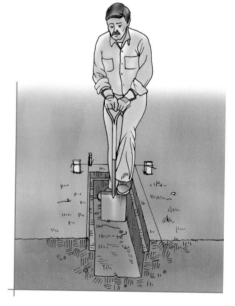

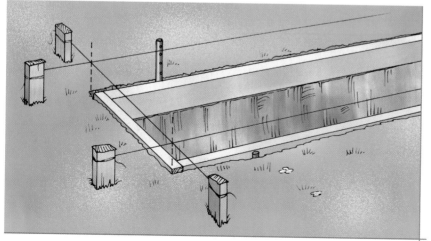

2 **FRAME THE FOOTING.** Cut 2 × 4s for the frame, then screw them together at the corners. Check for square and level in all directions. Drive metal stakes to anchor the frame; 2 × 4 stakes could cause the walls of the excavation to crumble. Drive the stakes below the top of the 2 × 4s.

3 **INSTALL REBAR.** Local building codes may call for reinforcement bar, which increases the footing's ability to resist cracking if the soil underneath shifts. Typically, two horizontal pieces of ⅜-inch rebar are sufficient. To suspend the rebar in the center of the footing's depth, drive vertical pieces of rebar into the ground and wire the horizontal pieces to them.

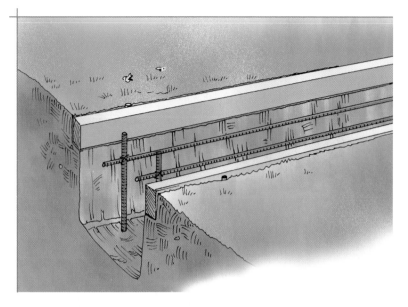

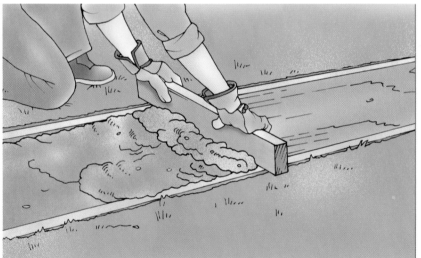

4 **POUR AND SCREED.** Mix concrete (see pages 90–91) and pour it into the hole. A basic concrete mix works fine. Use a length of 2 × 4 to screed the top. Smooth the concrete with a magnesium or wood float.

Framing a Step-Down

If the site is sloped, you may need to step down the footing. Construct two frames, one for the upper level and one for the lower level, and fasten them together with pieces of plywood.

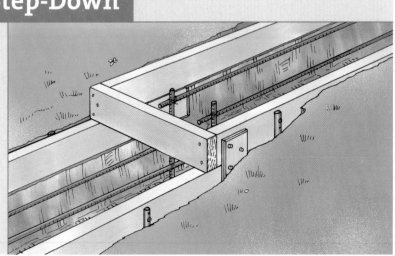

MORTARED STONE WALL

WHEN A LOW GARDEN WALL DOUBLES AS A BENCH, there's a good reason to build it with mortar. The mixture of cement, sand, and lime keeps the stones from jiggling loose, and it allows for efficient use of materials, as small stones or even chunks of old concrete can be used to fill in the center.

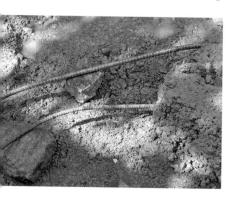

Jeffrey Bale, a stoneworker known for pebble mosaics (see pages 72–73), built the wall shown here to enclose a planting bed. Because he also planned to build a patio with 5-inch-thick concrete pavers along the front of the wall, he was able to prepare a compacted gravel base under the entire area and pour the wall foundation directly on that. He didn't need to excavate further for the foundation, because soil would be built up on one side and the paving on the other.

1 **INSTALL GRAVEL AND REBAR.** Excavate the area that will be under the wall, plus any adjoining area that you plan to pave. For a low, 2-foot-high wall like this, dig down at least 4 inches where winters are mild, or deeper where the soil freezes. Spread compactible gravel, dampen the surface with a soft spray from a hose, and tamp the gravel firm with a vibrating plate compactor. Place several lengths of ³⁄₈-inch rebar along the base of the wall. Shape gentle curves by bending the rebar by hand.

2 **MIX AND POUR THE FOUNDATION.** Prepare a bagged concrete mix with just enough water so it holds together and has little slump (see pages 86–87). Starting at one end of the wall, spread about half the batch 2 inches deep, then pull the rebar to the top and add 2 more inches of concrete. (If the soil slopes and you want a level top on the wall, pour enough concrete to build up the low areas, let that set, then pour the 4-inch-thick main foundation.

3 **SUPPORT THE REBAR.** To keep the rebar elevated about halfway within the foundation, you may wish to stick stones or other material underneath.

4 **ADD INTERIOR STONES.** As you form the foundation, place damp stones along one side of the wall. Bale forms the interior side of this planter wall with free chunks of salvaged concrete.

5 **PLACE FACE STONES.** Place stones along the most visible face of the wall. The stones should fit well enough so that the wall would stay intact even without mortar. Set small stones and chunks of concrete in the interior and pack mortar into gaps.

6 **ADD LAYERS.** Gradually build up the height of the wall by spreading a little mortar on a lower stone and then topping that with a new, damp piece. Try to follow the basic stonemason's rule of placing two stones over one or one over two, so that joints don't line up. Every 6 to 8 feet, select a large tie stone and orient it so that it extends through the entire thickness of the wall or at least well into the middle.

7 **PLACE CAPSTONES.** When you get to the top layer, set blocky pieces with a wide, flat face. To create a level surface on top, support pieces underneath with smaller stones and a little mortar where necessary. Trial-fit pieces so that they also fit well together on the top. Once you mortar them in place, you should see only a thin, relatively uniform mortar joint between them. As you set each capstone in mortar, check that the top is as level as possible and that the height lines up with that of adjoining stones.

8 **CLEAN THE SURFACE.** Use a masonry cleaner as directed on the label to remove the thin film of cement from the stones. Bale uses muriatic acid, so he wears a respirator fitted with acid-gas cartridges, as well as goggles and acid-resistant gloves. When the stones look clean, wash off the residue with water from a garden hose.

FAUX DRY-STACKED WALL

BY PACKING MORTAR OR CONCRETE INTO THE CENTER, you can build a stone wall that looks dry-stacked but has the solid feel of a mortared wall. It's an ideal solution where people will sit on the wall or where you are building with relatively small stones.

Pat Knight, a stonemason and landscaper near Seattle, uses the method shown here. It's basically a thin dry-stacked wall on the perimeter, filled in at the center with concrete and chunks of stone or recycled concrete. There is no foundation other than compacted gravel.

Where winters are cold enough for the ground to freeze, build the bottom portion of the wall as a true dry-stacked wall, without leaving a hollow area in the center (see pages 124–125). When you get to the top foot or so, add mortar between stones, but keep it well back from the face so it doesn't show. This allows the bottom portion of the wall to flex a bit as the ground freezes and thaws. Inspect the capstone layer each year and repair any cracks that have occurred in the mortar.

The wall shown here is 6 feet long, 28 inches deep, and 18 inches high, a great height for a bench. If you are building a wall as a serving area for food or drinks, you might want to add about 10 inches.

1 MARK THE PERIMETER AND EXCAVATE. Using spray paint or stakes and twine, mark the perimeter. For a curved wall, mark one long face and then measure out at several places so the opposite wall curves an equal distance away. Excavate with a flat shovel to a depth of 5 or 6 inches. Dig straight down on the perimeter.

2 ADD GRAVEL. Dump compactible gravel with particles ¾ inch and smaller into the excavation until it is 4 inches deep. For this job, the crew used basalt. Spread the gravel level with a rake, mist the material with water, and make several passes over it with a vibrating plate compactor. Then spread an inch or so of finer gravel, with particles 1.4 inches and smaller. Do not compact this layer. Keep it loose so you can move it as needed to adjust the height of the stones.

3 SET THE BASE LAYER. Select stones for the bottom course. Ideally, they should be relatively large and have at least two fairly flat faces that form a right angle. Use large, block-shaped stones for corners. Set the stones on the gravel and pack in the fine material, as needed, to make the stones stable. The front face should be as straight as possible and the top of each stone should be as level as possible. Stones should fit well together.

4 **TRIM STONES.** Where slight bulges keep stones from fitting well together, alter the stones using one of the techniques shown on pages 29–30. Here, a few taps on a stone chisel did the trick.

5 **BUILD UP THE CORNERS.** Begin the second course at the corners. Check the height so you don't set stones higher than you want the wall to be.

6 **ADD COURSES.** Continue to set stones around the perimeter. It's fine to have a ragged edge on the interior, with some stones projecting well into the space.

7 **ADD CONCRETE.** Prepare a basic concrete mix and pack it into the center of the wall. Fill in around crevices as you go; don't wait until the wall is full. To minimize the chance that the pressure of the wet concrete will push stones out of place, allow one layer to set before you add the next. This job took ¾ cubic yard of concrete.

8 **CREATE A LEVEL TOP.** When the concrete has set, place thin, flat shim stones along the perimeter as needed to establish a level line. Then prepare a mortar mix as directed on the bag. Using the shim stones as a height guide, trowel the mortar over the top of the wall to create a level base for the capstones. Trowel it smooth, then scratch it up with a notched trowel so the final mortar layer will stick better.

9 **SET THE CAPSTONES.** Select thick, flat stones for the top layer and trim them as needed so they fit well together and extend out from the sides by an inch or two. Working from a cardboard or plywood template will speed this step and save you from a lot of heavy lifting. When all the pieces are ready, prepare a fresh batch of mortar, trowel some of it on top of the wall, and set each capstone straight down into the mortar. Check with a level and tamp down with a rubber mallet as needed. Fill and smooth any joints between stones. Wipe away any mortar spills with a damp sponge.

BRICK GARDEN WALL

LOW, SHORT GARDEN WALLS CAN BE BUILT WITH A SINGLE WYTHE—that is, with only one horizontal row of bricks. But such walls are not strong. You can even push them over by hand. Double-wythe brick walls are much stronger, though if they are more than 2 feet high, they may not be strong enough to act as retaining walls.

Brick walls must rest atop a solid concrete footing (see pages 126–127).

Patterns, called bonds, allow you to build double-wythe walls that interlock in various ways. Bricks turned sideways to tie the wythes together are called headers, while the rest of the bricks are stretchers. Most bonds require cutting. To help you maintain rhythm and concentration as you throw mortar and lay bricks, cut a number of bricks ahead of time. For cutting techniques, see pages 28–29.

Working with Mortar

A professional mason can throw a neat line of mortar at just the right thickness with ease and speed. Don't expect to equal that after a couple of hours of practice. But you can learn to throw mortar well enough to construct a straight wall with neat joints. See page 66 for tips about selecting the best mortar. Type N is usually fine. Mix mortar with a hoe or shovel in a wheelbarrow or mortar tray, or use a paddle mixer in a large plastic tub. You can scoop mortar out of the mixing container, but it's often easier to load a shovelful onto a hawk or a piece of plywood about 16 inches square and work from there.

Make up about one-third of a bag of mortar mix with just enough water so it's thick enough to hold its shape when you cut ridges in it with a mason's trowel. If you scoop up some mortar with the trowel and hold it upside down, the mortar should stick to the trowel for a second or two. Here's how to practice your technique.

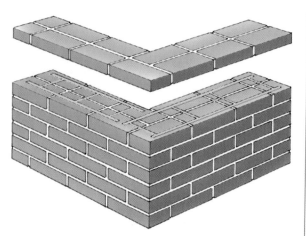

Running bond has no headers and doesn't require you to cut bricks. Embed metal reinforcement in the mortar every four or five courses. Use ladder-type reinforcement, as shown, or push corrugated wall ties into the mortar every foot or so.

Common bond, also known as American bond, uses headers every fifth course and requires a small amount of extra cutting.

1 **THROW A LINE.** Scoop up mortar with the trowel. With the face of the trowel pointing up, snap the trowel downward quickly. The mortar will lift very slightly and make a smacking sound as it settles back onto the trowel. This loosens the mortar's grip on the trowel.

Next comes the tricky part. To throw a line of mortar, extend your arm so that the trowel is at the point farthest from you. Rotate the trowel until mortar starts to slide off, then pull the trowel back toward you. The goal is to deposit mortar in an even line about 1 inch thick, three-quarters of a brick wide, and two or three bricks long. The process should be quick and smooth.

2 **FURROW THE MORTAR.** Drag the trowel through the mortar to produce a channel about half the thickness of the mortar line. If mortar slides off the side of the bricks, slice it off as shown in step 5.

3 **BUTTER A BRICK END.** Every brick, except the first one in a course, needs to have at least one end buttered. Hold the brick in one hand and load the trowel with a small amount of mortar. Scrape the trowel at a 45-degree angle to the brick end and then lightly pull the trowel back. Shape the mortar in this way in all four directions.

4 **PUSH A BRICK INTO PLACE.** Set the brick on the mortar bed, about 2 inches away from the brick it will abut, and slide it into place. Ideally, a little mortar will squeeze out of all the joints. Any small gaps at the joints can be filled in when you tool the joint (see step 7, page 135). If there are gaps greater than an inch, remove the brick and start again.

If a brick sits too high, tap it down using the handle of the trowel. If it's too low, do not pull it upward, as that would create a weak joint. Remove the brick, scrape off the mortar, and start again.

5 **SLICE OFF THE EXCESS.** Use the trowel like a knife to slice off the squeezed-out mortar. If you slice quickly and in one motion, little mortar will smear onto the face of the bricks. Every 10 minutes or so, depending on the heat and humidity, strike and perhaps clean the joints.

Building a Brick Wall

Before you start laying bricks, make a story pole so you can quickly measure bricks for the correct height. Lay a number of bricks with ³/₈-inch spaces between them, on edge on a flat surface. Then lay a length of 1 × 2 or 1 × 4 next to the bricks and draw marks indicating the centers of each mortar joint. Alternatively, purchase a ready-made story pole. A standard model has marks every 8 inches to indicate three courses of common brick plus the mortar joints.

1 **LAY A DRY RUN.** Snap chalk lines on the footing indicating the outline of the wall. Place the bricks on the footing in a dry run, with ³/₈-inch dowels between them to represent the joints. Make sure you understand how the bricks will be laid out at the corner. You might need to cut a brick or two. You may choose to minimize cutting by moving one wall over an inch or two. With a pencil, mark the footing for the centers of each joint.

2 **LAY THE FIRST BRICKS.** Remove the dry-laid bricks. Starting at a corner or at the end of a wall, throw a line of mortar for the first three bricks. Set and place the first brick. Butter one end of the other bricks and set them. Push the bricks into place and see that the centers of the joints are at the pencil marks. Use a level to check that the bricks form an even surface in both directions. Scrape away excess mortar. Repeat for the second wythe and lay bricks for the start of an adjoining wall if you are at a corner.

3 **LAY A HEADER COURSE.** Be sure you understand how the bricks must be stacked. As you stack, every now and then hold a level against the joints to see that they line up vertically. For common bond, a header course needs two three-quarter bricks and two one-quarter bricks, known as closures, at each corner. Scrape away excess mortar as you go. Every so often, check the joints to see if they need to be struck (see step 7).

4 **BUILD A LEAD.** Continue building the corner or the end of the wall, which is called a lead. Make a stack seven or eight bricks high. As you go, use a level to check that the corner is plumb and the courses level. Use a story pole to check joint thickness. Do not slide bricks to adjust their position, unless you have laid them within the past two minutes.

5 **STRING A LINE BETWEEN LEADS.** Build a lead at the other end of the wall in the same way and check it with the story pole and level. Lay all the in-between bricks for the bottom course of both wythes, using the pencil lines as guides. Hook mason's blocks and stretch a mason's line from one lead to the other at the center of a joint. The line should be taut and about ⅛ inch from the bricks.

6 **FILL IN BETWEEN THE LEADS.** For each course, move the line blocks up one joint and use the line as a guide for the height and for the outer edge of the wall. Don't let bricks touch the line. The last brick in the middle of a course, called the closure brick, is buttered at both ends. Butter it generously and slip it in straight down. Avoid sliding it. You may need to use a striking tool to force more mortar into one joint.

7 **STRIKE THE JOINTS.** Every 20 minutes or so, depending on weather conditions, test the joints by pressing with your thumb. If a thumbprint holds its shape, it's time to strike. With a brick jointer, smooth all horizontal joints, then smooth the verticals so water will drain properly. If a bit of mortar oozes out from the jointing tool, leave it or it will smear.

8 **BRUSH AND CLEAN.** Brush off excess mortar once it has started to harden and appears crumbly. If the mortar smears, stop and wait a few minutes longer. You may be able to wipe any smears away with a damp sponge, but take care not to get the joints very wet or you will weaken them. Alternatively, wait a day and then clean with a mild muriatic acid solution.

CONCRETE-BLOCK WALL

MANY CONCRETE-BLOCK WALLS ARE MADE WITH BLOCKS SET IN MORTAR BEDS, much like a brick wall. But there are easier options: decorative interlocking blocks, which form a finished wall as soon as they are stacked, and surface-bonded concrete blocks, which consist of standard or special blocks that are stacked dry and then stuccoed with special material.

Decorative interlocking blocks suitable for forming freestanding, vertical walls may require different installation methods than the interlocking blocks used for retaining walls (see page 121). Some stackable blocks can be set on a compacted gravel base, while others require a solid concrete footing. Discuss your needs with a salesperson at a masonry-supply company and read the instructions before you buy materials.

Surface-Bonded Block Walls

Concrete-block walls built without mortar may sound flimsy, but when coated with surface-bonding cement, they are actually stronger than walls built the conventional way. The surface-bonding cement, which is sold in bags along

with other concrete mixes, contains fiber reinforcement as well as cement, fine sand, and polymers. You can buy special interlocking concrete blocks, or use standard ones for walls shorter than 3 feet or so. A surface-bonded wall must rest on a solid concrete foundation (see pages 126–127). Check with your local building department about whether you need a permit and whether there are local requirements for internal reinforcement.

1 **MAKE CUTS.** After the concrete footing has cured, set a row of blocks in a dry run. Make any necessary cuts by scoring a line about $1/2$ inch deep on each side with a circular saw fitted with a masonry or diamond blade. Finish the cut with a sledge hammer. Snap chalk lines to indicate the perimeter.

2 **LAY THE FIRST COURSE.** Mix a batch of surface-bonding cement and dampen the foundation. Where the blocks will go, spread the bonding cement as deep as the manufacturer recommends, often $1/8$ inch to $1/2$ inch. Set the first course in that. Use a solid-faced block at the end. Check the alignment with a level.

3 **STACK THE BLOCKS.** Stack the next courses so joints line up every other course. Use a mason's line and level to check the wall as you go. If it's required by code, fill cores with an approved grout.

4 **SHIM WHERE NEEDED.** If a block wobbles, stack the next course. If the weight of the blocks doesn't solve the problem, pick up the upper course, as well as the wobbly block. Trowel mortar on top of the block below and set the wobbly block back into place. Tap with a hammer and a scrap of wood to settle the block at the same height as its neighbors.

5 **CAP THE WALL.** For a square-shaped top, cap the wall with interlocking cap blocks. If these are not available, spread surface-bonding mortar on the highest course and lay solid concrete pavers on the mortar.

6 **APPLY SURFACE-BONDING MORTAR.** Spray the wall with water. Mix a small batch of surface-bonding cement and place it on a hawk. Hold the hawk against the wall and trowel the cement upward. With the trowel nearly flat, press firmly to ensure a tight bond.

7 **SMOOTH THE SURFACE AND MAKE CONTROL JOINTS.** Once you have covered an area about 4 feet square, use long, sweeping strokes to smooth the surface. The cement should be about ¼ inch thick. Rinse the trowel regularly, as a clean trowel is easier to use. To control cracking, use a concrete jointer to cut vertical control joints spaced about twice as far apart as the wall's height. (Space them 6 feet apart on a 3-foot-high wall.) Create a subtle texture by lightly running the trowel over the surface in sweeping motions. When applied lightly, a texture will not affect the control joints.

INSTALLING STONE VENEER

A THIN STONE COVERING IS ANOTHER WAY TO DRESS UP A WALL of concrete, block, or brick. Use thin flagstones or shop for stone cut specifically to be thin wall material. Known as thin natural veneer, it shows the edge detail on stone rather than the face that you'd normally see in paving. The veneer products may also have special corner pieces, which you can use to create wall ends, posts, or corners that don't show the thin edge of the stones.

Working with thin, lightweight veneer is a breeze compared with building stone walls or even installing veneers of thicker materials. You can cut pieces with a tile saw or brick saw, and you don't need a foundation or metal ties to connect the wall to the veneer. You just stick the veneer up, let the mortar dry, then fill the joints with grout.

The wall itself should be in sound condition. Clean away any oily deposits. If you see the white powder known as efflorescence, correct the underlying moisture problem and scrub away the minerals first with a stiff brush.

CONSTRUCTION TIP

Many types of veneer can be installed from the top down, which reduces mortar smears. To test, butter the back of a sample with mortar and press the piece onto a concrete block. If the sample slips, start at the bottom. Layered stone should always be installed from the bottom up, or it won't look right.

1 **LAY THE STONES IN A DRY RUN.** Lay a sheet of plywood, as wide as the wall is tall, on the ground near the wall, and place it so that you can easily pick up stones from the plywood and apply them to the wall. Lay stones on the plywood in a dry run as they will appear on the wall. If you are using corner pieces, place them first so you don't have to cut them. Corner pieces have a long and a short side. Alternate the sides as you go up the wall. Make any necessary cuts (see pages 28–30).

2 **APPLY MORTAR TO THE WALL.** Spread a coat of concrete bonding agent onto the wall. Mix a batch of mortar with a hoe or shovel in a wheelbarrow or mortar tray, or use a paddle mixer in a plastic tub. The mortar should be stiff but just wet enough to stick to the stones. Use a straight trowel to apply the mortar to the wall. Aim for a coat about 3/8 inch thick—or thicker if the stones are not flat. Cover an area of about 15 square feet.

3 **SET THE BOTTOM ROW OF STONES.** Mist the back of the stones with water so they bond better. Starting at the bottom, press pieces into the mortar. Where necessary, use blocks of wood or small rocks to hold them in position. Make all adjustments as soon as possible. Avoid moving a stone after the mortar has begun to harden.

4 **SET THE UPPER STONES.** If the stones are light enough, continue setting them up to the top of the wall. However, if the weight of the upper stones causes lower ones to slide, wait for the mortar under the lower stones to set. Continue to use spacers to maintain fairly consistent joints. Every 10 minutes or so, pull a stone off the wall and check the back to make sure at least three-quarters of the surface shows mortar stains. If necessary, back-butter the stones with mortar before setting them.

5 **FILL AND STRIKE THE JOINTS.** After the mortar has stiffened, go back and fill in the joints with mortar. Use a pointed trowel or a mortar bag to slip and press mortar into the joints. Wipe the trowel or bag tip with a damp towel and rinse it often. When the mortar starts to stiffen, strike and brush the joints.

6 **CAP AND CLEAN THE WALL.** At the top of the wall, install large stones that overhang by an inch or more on each side. When the mortar has started to harden, wash the wall with water and a brush, then wipe it with a wet towel. If you are using artificial stone veneer, brush off mortar spills after the mortar dries a bit.

CREDITS

DESIGNERS
1: Cording Landscape Design; 3 top: Roger's Gardens; 4 top: Rob Steiner; 4 bottom left: Michelle Derviss; 4 bottom right: Duncan Callicott; 5 bottom right: Bud Stuckey; 6 bottom left: Teri Ravel Kane, Landscape Architect and Vicente Chavez, concrete; 6 top: Amy Korn and Matt Randolph, KornRandolph; 7 top: Dan Borroff Landscape; 7 bottom left and right: Dahlin Group Architecture and Planning, McDonald & Moore Interior Design, Nuvis Landscape Architecture and Planning; 8 top: Huettl-Thuilot Associates; 9 bottom right: Conni Cross; 9 bottom left: Duncan Callicott; 9 top: Tito Patri; 13 bottom: Richard Wogisch; 16: David Yakish; 17 right: Pat Nordquist, Artisans Concrete Supply; 18 bottom: Michelle Derviss; 19 middle: Tom Pellett; 19 top: Michael Glassman & Associates; 20 bottom left: Dan Borroff Landscape; 20 top right: Neumann Mendro Andrulaitis Architects; 22 bottom: Gail Gee; 22 top: Barbara Jackel Landscape Design; 22 middle: Bud Stuckey; 25 top: Teri Ravel Kane, Landscape Architect and Vicente Chavez, concrete; 32 bottom right: Richard Wogisch; 32 bottom left: Dan Messina & Conni Cross; 32 bottom middle: Conni Cross; 32 top: Hillary Curtis & David Thorne, David Thorne Landscape Architects; 33 bottom right and 34 left: Paul Harris, Imagine Sonoma; 34 right: Tito Patri and Jefferson Mack Metal; 35 bottom left: Roger's Gardens; 35 bottom right: Andrea Cochran Landscape Architecture; 48 top left: Tom Pellet; 54: Paul Harris, Imagine Sonoma; 60 top left: Judy Ogden; 60 bottom: Landscapes by Atlantic; 61 top: Richard Wogisch; 61 bottom right: Conni Cross; 76 left and right: Monika Hellwegen and Azul Cobb, Carlotta from Paradise; 77 top: Isabelle Clara Greene, Landscape Architect, F.A.S.L.A.; 79 top: Dan Borroff Landscape; 79 bottom right: Dan Messina & Conni Cross; 82 top: Luis Llenza Garden Design; 84 bottom left: Isabelle Clara Greene, Landscape Architect, F.A.S.L.A.; 84 bottom right: Katherine Greenberg; 84 top: Benjamin H. Hammontree; 114 bottom right: Richard Wogisch; 114 top: Kristina Kessel & David Thorne, David Thorne Landscape Architects; 115 bottom right: Conni Cross; 116 top: Bob Clark; 117 bottom right: Bill Smith; 119 top: Conni Cross; 120: Suzanne Porter

Resources

LANDSCAPERS AND OTHER CONTRACTORS

Artisans Concrete Supply
Keyport, WA
(360) 509-8651

Azteca Decorative Concrete
Kingston, WA
(360) 271-0566

Jeffrey Bale Garden Design
Portland, OR
www.jeffreygardens.com

Botanica, Inc.
Bainbridge Island, WA
(206) 842-2820

Olive Branch Landscape Inc.
Kingston, WA
(360) 297-7282

Plantswoman Design
Bainbridge Island, WA
www.plantswomandesign.com
(206) 842-2453

Barbara Schmidt Landscape Design Inc.
Hansfille, WA
www.barbaraschmidt.com
(360) 638-1211

BUILDING MATERIALS
A.M. Leonard, Inc.
amleo.com
(800) 543-8955
Non-motorized sod cutters

Colormaker Floors Ltd.
www.colormakerfloors.com
(888) 875-9425
Tools and materials for topping concrete

Cultured Stone®
www.culturedstone.com
Artificial stone

Decorative Concrete Supplies
www.decrete.com
(866) 332-7383
Stencils for concrete

Oly-Ola Edgings Inc.
www.olyola.com
(630) 833-3033
Edging

L.M. Scofield Co.
www.scofield.com
(800) 800-9900
Color hardener for concrete

Muck-Truck
www.mucktruckusa.com
(772) 461-7880
Motorized wheelbarrow

Mule Creek Adobe, New Mexico
www.mulecreekadobe.com
(505) 535-2973
Adobe block

Mutual Materials
www.mutualmaterials.com
(800) 477-3008
Masonry and hardscape products

Robinson Brick
www.robinsonbrick.com
(800) 477-9002
Brick and thin true stone veneer

StampMaster/Creative Urethane Concepts Inc.
www.stampmaster.net
(803) 376-4430
Stamps for concrete

Watsontown Brick Co.
www.watsontownbrick.com
(800) 538-204
Brick

INDEX

A

acid stains, 16, 104
acrylic fortifiers, 86, 89
adhesives, bonding, 68, 86, 112–113
adobe blocks, 20
aggregate
  component of concrete, 16, 86
  exposed, 17, 110–111
angled cuts, 29, 31
ashlar stone, 11

B

backfill
  edging, 47
  retaining wall, 122–123
Bale, Jeffrey (mosaic artist), 69,
  72–73, 128–129
bark, shredded, 19
base preparation, 42–43
basket weave patterns, 60, 64
batter gauge, 124
batterboards, 38–39
blocks
  adobe, 20
  concrete, 15, 136–137
  cutting techniques, 28, 136
  walls, 121, 136–137
bonding adhesives, 68, 86, 112–113
border cuts, 31
brick splitter, 28
bricks, 12–13
  buttering, 133
  colored, 12
  concrete, 13
  cutting, 28
  "frogged", 13
  mortared, 66–67
  patio, 58–65
  patterns, 60–61
  paving, 12, 66–67
  tilted edging, 51
  used, 13
  veneer, 13
  walk, 58–65
  walls, 12, 132–135
broom finish, 103
building permits, 24
bull floats, 102

C

calculations
  concrete, 88
  for materials, 26
  stairway, 78–79
capstones, 125, 129, 131, 137,
  139
carrying techniques, 26–27
catch basins, 45
cement
  component of concrete, 16, 86
  safety, 92
ceramic tile, 18
cobblestones
  concrete, 14
  natural, 11
  patio/walk, 58–65
color in concrete, 16, 103, 104
compaction of gravel, 43
compactor, vibrating plate
  base preparation, 55
  flagstones, 57
  flagstones on concrete, 69
  pavers, 63
concrete, 86–92
  assessing moisture content,
    86, 87
  bricks, 13
  calculating needs, 88
  cobblestones, 14
  crack prevention, 88–89
  decoding bagged mixes, 87
  decorative effects, 94–95, 104–111
  delivery options, 90, 91
  demolishing old, 40
  disposal of waste, 100
  edging, 52–53
  edging mortared into, 53
  footings, 126–127
  freeze-resistant, 89
  mixing options, 90–91
  old meets new, 99
  overlays, 112–113
  patio, 96–103
  paver ensembles, 60
  pavers, 14
  poured, 16–17
  scratch recipes, 92
  shrinkage, 89
  slump test, 86
  steppingstones, 93
  versatility, 84–85
  walk, 94–95

concrete blocks
  blocks, 15
  wall, 121, 136–137
concrete mixers, 90–91
construction methods, 9
control joints, 102, 137
cost, 8–9, 20
crack prevention in concrete, 88–89
crushed stone, 19
curved wood edging, 48, 96–98
curves
  corner, 39
  layout, 36, 38
  walks, 65
cutting techniques, 28–31
  angles, 29, 31
  concrete block, 136
  pavers, 75
  saltillos, 71

D

darby, 102
decorative concrete blocks, 15
decorative effects in concrete,
  104–111
demolition, concrete, 40
design
  brick and paver patterns, 72
  grid patterns, 60–61
  hardscape as structural element,
    6–7
  mixing materials, 20
  options in concrete, 84–85
  pebble mosaic, 72–73, 93
  with steppingstones, 36
  walls, 119
drainage
  for pervious paving, 74
  puddling, 54, 74
  solutions, 44–45
  wall, 121
drum roller, 55
dry wells, 45
dry-stacked stone walls, 122–123,
  124–125, 130–131

E

edges, rounded, 102
edging
  concrete, 52–53
  curved, 48, 96–98
  invisible, 46

7/18/08 ♦ Hf